PRENTICE Realidades

Practice Workbook
with Writing, Audio
& Video Activities

PEARSON

Prentice
Hall

Boston, Massachusetts
Upper Saddle River, New Jersey

ISBN 0-13-116461-9

18   16

Practice Workbook

¿Cómo te llamas?

It is the first day of school in Madrid, and students are getting to know each other. Complete the dialogues by circling the appropriate words and phrases.

1. **A:** ¡Hola! (Hasta luego. / ¿Cómo te llamas?)

    B: Me llamo Rubén. ¿Y tú?

    A: Me llamo Antonio.

    B: (Mucho gusto. / Bien, gracias.)

    A: Igualmente, Rubén.

2. It is 9:00 in the morning.

    A: (¡Buenas tardes! / ¡Buenos días!) ¿Cómo te llamas?

    B: Buenos días. Me llamo Rosalía. ¿Cómo te llamas tú?

    A: Me llamo Enrique. (¿Cómo estás, Rosalía? / Gracias, Rosalía.)

    B: Muy bien, gracias. ¿Y tú?

    A: (Encantado. / Bien.)

    B: Adiós, Enrique.

    A: (¡Sí! / ¡Nos vemos!)

3. It is now 2:00 P.M.

    A: ¡Buenas tardes, Sr. Gómez!

    B: (¡Buenas noches! / ¡Buenas tardes!) ¿Cómo te llamas?

    A: Me llamo Margarita.

    B: Mucho gusto, Margarita.

    A: (Buenos días. / Encantada.) ¡Adiós, Sr. Gómez!

    B: (¡Hasta luego! / ¡Bien!)

¿Eres formal o informal?

A. Circle the phrases below that can be used to talk to teachers. Underline the phrases that can be used to talk to other students. Some phrases may be both circled and underlined.

¡Hola!	¿Cómo está Ud.?	Mucho gusto.	¿Qué tal?
Buenos días.	¿Cómo estás?	¿Y usted?	¡Hasta luego!
¡Nos vemos!	Buenos días, señor.	Estoy bien.	¿Y tú?

B. Circle **Ud.** or **tú** to indicate how you would address the person being spoken to.

1. "Hola, Sr. Gómez." **Ud.** **Tú**

2. "¿Qué tal, Luis?" **Ud.** **Tú**

3. "¿Cómo estás, Paco?" **Ud.** **Tú**

4. "¡Buenos días, profesor!" **Ud.** **Tú**

5. "Adiós, señora." **Ud.** **Tú**

C. Number the following phrases from 1–5 to create a logical conversation. Number 1 should indicate the first thing that was said, and 5 should indicate the last thing that was said.

_____ Bien, gracias, ¿y Ud.?

_____ ¡Hasta luego!

_____ Buenas tardes.

_____ ¡Buenas tardes! ¿Cómo está Ud.?

_____ Muy bien. ¡Adiós!

Realidades **A**

Para empezar

En la escuela

Nombre _____

Fecha _____

Hora _____

Practice Workbook **P–3**

Por favor

Your Spanish teacher has asked you to learn some basic classroom commands. Write the letter of the appropriate phrase next to the picture it corresponds to.

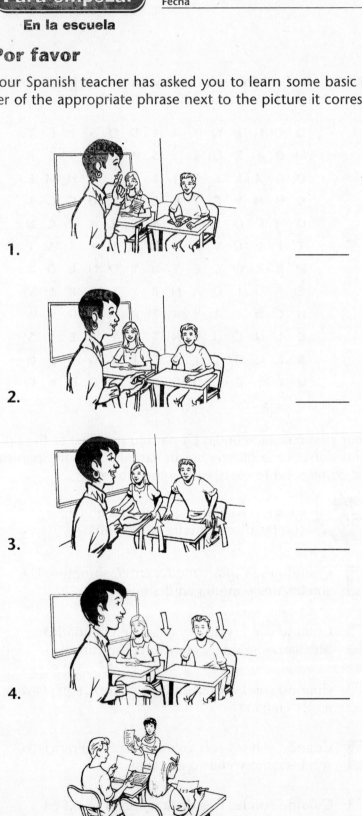

1. _____

2. _____

3. _____

4. _____

5. _____

A. Saquen una hoja de papel.

B. Siéntense, por favor.

C. Repitan, por favor.

D. ¡Silencio, por favor!

E. Levántense, por favor.

Realidades (A)

Para empezar

En la escuela

Nombre _____

Hora _____

Fecha _____

Practice Workbook **P–4**

Los números

A. Here are some simple math problems. First, fill in each blank with the correct number. Then, find the Spanish word for that number in the word search to the right.

1. $7 \times 8 =$ _____

2. 50, 40, _____ , 20, 10 . . .

3. $75 + 7 =$ _____

4. 55, 60, 65, _____ , 75, 80 . . .

5. 97, 98, 99, _____ . . .

6. $24 \div 2 =$ _____

7. 72, 60, _____ , 36, 24 . . .

```
O C H E N T A Y D O S L C T
M O J X U E Y S W H U S S R
O G X L E G I L E C E H M E
G U N V C T B C R T U C G I
O H C O Y A T N E R A U C N
T T C C V A T N W L Y F W T
M B K W C E T U Y O N L O A
E F Q F Q A N B Y F K R L V
H C E E A Y R T D M W D A W
C I N C U E N T A Y S E I S
R E C O J I W C J Y G Q U Q
U L J D I U D G V X D D K G
```

B. As exchange students, you and your classmates are finding it hard to get used to the time difference. Below are some statements about time differences in various U.S and Spanish-speaking cities. Write in the times that correspond to each. Follow the model.

Modelo `10:30` `10:30` Cuando son las diez y media en Chicago, son las diez y media en Panamá.

1.  Cuando es la una y media en Washington, D.C., son las dos y media en Buenos Aires.

2.  Cuando son las doce y cuarto en Ciudad de México, es la una y cuarto en San Juan.

3.  Cuando son las diez en Nueva York, son las diez en La Habana.

4.  Cuando son las seis y cuarto en San Francisco, son las ocho y cuarto en Lima.

5.  Cuando son las dos de la mañana (*A.M.*) en Madrid, son las siete de la tarde (*P.M.*) en Bogotá.

Go Online WEB CODE jcd-0002
PHSchool.com

Realidades Ⓐ

Para empezar

En la escuela

Nombre _____

Fecha _____

Hora _____

Practice Workbook **P–5**

El cuerpo

A. You are watching your neighbor's toddler Anita for a few hours after school. She is playing with her **muñequita** (*doll*) Chula and is practicing words to identify body parts. Help her by drawing lines to connect her doll's body parts with their correct names.

el ojo   la boca

el dedo   el estómago

la nariz

la mano

el brazo   el pie

la cabeza   la pierna

B. Now write three sentences using the phrase **me duele** and body parts.

1. _____

2. _____

3. _____

Realidades Ⓐ

Para empezar

En la clase

Nombre _____

Hora _____

Fecha _____

Practice Workbook **P–6**

Combinaciones

A. Write the correct article (**el** or **la**, or both) before each of the items below.

1. _____ bolígrafo
2. _____ lápiz
3. _____ sala de clases
4. _____ profesora
5. _____ cuaderno

6. _____ carpeta
7. _____ profesor
8. _____ estudiante
9. _____ pupitre
10. _____ hoja de papel

B. To make sure that there are enough school supplies for everyone, your teacher has asked you to help take inventory. Complete each sentence by writing the number and name of each item pictured. Follow the model.

Modelo   veinticinco   No hay un _*libro*_. Hay _25_____.

1. sesenta y siete   No hay un _____. Hay _____.

2. cien   No hay un _____. Hay _____.

3. veintiuno   No hay un _____. Hay _____.

4. diecinueve   No hay un _____. Hay _____.

5. treinta y seis   No hay un _____. Hay _____.

Go Online WEB CODE jcd-0004
PHSchool.com

Realidades Ⓐ

Para empezar

En la clase

Nombre _____

Fecha _____

Hora _____

Practice Workbook **P–7**

El calendario

February has just ended on a leap year. Because of this, Pepe is completely lost in planning out March. Help him get his days straight by using the calendar. Follow the model.

lunes	martes	miércoles	jueves	viernes	sábado	domingo
				1	2	3
4	5	6	7	8	9	10
11	12	13	14	15	16	17
18	19	20	21	22	23	24
25	26	27	28	29	30	31

Modelo   TÚ: Hoy es el cinco de marzo.

PEPE: ¿Es jueves?

TÚ: No, es martes.

1. TÚ: Hoy es el treinta de marzo.

PEPE: ¿Es lunes?

TÚ: _____

2. TÚ: Hoy es el trece de marzo.

PEPE: ¿Es domingo?

TÚ: _____

3. TÚ: Hoy es el veintiuno de marzo.

PEPE: ¿Es domingo?

TÚ: _____

4. TÚ: Hoy es el once de marzo.

PEPE: ¿Es miércoles?

TÚ: _____

5. TÚ: Hoy es el primero de marzo.

PEPE: ¿Es martes?

TÚ: _____

6. TÚ: Hoy es el doce de marzo.

PEPE: ¿Es sábado?

TÚ: _____

7. TÚ: Hoy es el veinticuatro de marzo.

PEPE: ¿Es viernes?

TÚ: _____

8. TÚ: Hoy es el diecisiete de marzo.

PEPE: ¿Es lunes?

TÚ: _____

La fecha

A. Write out the following dates in Spanish. The first one is done for you.

Día/Mes

2/12   *el dos de diciembre* _____

9/3   _____

5/7   _____

4/9   _____

8/11   _____

1/1   _____

> **¿Recuerdas?**
>
> Remember that when writing the date in Spanish, the day precedes the month.
>
> • 19/12 = el 19 de diciembre = December 19
> • 27/3 = el 27 de marzo = March 27

B. Now, answer the following questions about dates in complete sentences.

1. ¿Cuál es la fecha de hoy?

_____

2. ¿El Día de San Valentín es el trece de enero?

_____

3. ¿Cuál es la fecha del Año Nuevo?

_____

4. ¿La Navidad (*Christmas*) es el 25 de noviembre?

_____

5. ¿Cuál es la fecha del Día de San Patricio?

_____

6. ¿Cuál es la fecha del Día de la Independencia?

_____

7. ¿Cuál es la fecha de mañana?

_____

Realidades (A)

Para empezar

El tiempo

Nombre _____

Fecha _____

Hora _____

Practice Workbook **P–9**

¿Qué tiempo hace?

You and several Spanish-speaking exchange students are discussing the weather of your home countries.

A. Fill in the chart with the missing information for the area in which you live.

Meses	Estación	Tiempo
diciembre enero _____	_____	_____
marzo _____ _____	_____	_____
junio _____ _____	verano	_____
_____ _____ noviembre	_____	hace viento, hace sol

B. Complete the dialogues below with information from the chart.

1. PROFESORA: ¿Qué tiempo hace en julio?

   ESTUDIANTE: _____

2. PROFESORA: ¿En enero hace calor?

   ESTUDIANTE: _____

3. PROFESORA: ¿En qué meses hace frío?

   ESTUDIANTE: _____

4. PROFESORA: ¿Qué tiempo hace en el verano?

   ESTUDIANTE: _____

5. PROFESORA: ¿Nieva en agosto?

   ESTUDIANTE: _____

Realidades Ⓐ

Para empezar

Nombre _____

Fecha _____

Hora _____

Practice Workbook **P–10**

Repaso

Fill in the crossword puzzle with the Spanish translation of the English words given below.

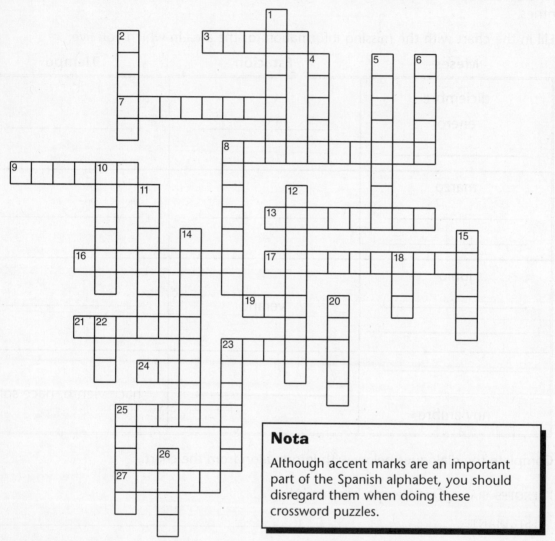

Nota

Although accent marks are an important part of the Spanish alphabet, you should disregard them when doing these crossword puzzles.

Across

3. pencil
7. season
8. See you later!
9. it is raining
13. it is cold
16. winter
17. September
19. day
21. head
23. madam, Mrs.
24. foot
25. week
27. fall

Down

1. Friday
2. Monday
4. it is snowing
5. male teacher
6. January
8. it is sunny
10. summer
11. desk
12. it is hot
14. spring
15. the date
18. month
20. arm
22. year
23. Saturday
25. sir, Mr.
26. Hello

Organizer

I. Vocabulary

Greetings and good-byes

_____
_____
_____
_____

Words to talk about time

_____
_____
_____
_____

Classroom objects

_____
_____
_____
_____
_____

Phrases to talk about names

_____
_____

Forms of address (Formal)

_____
_____
_____

Forms of address (Informal)

_____

Body parts

_____
_____
_____
_____
_____
_____
_____

Phrases to ask and tell how you feel

_____
_____
_____
_____
_____

Realidades **A**

Para empezar

Nombre _____

Hora _____

Fecha _____

Practice Workbook **P–12**

Days of the week

_____

_____

_____

_____

_____

_____

Months of the year

_____

_____

_____

_____

_____

_____

_____

_____

_____

_____

_____

_____

Seasons

_____

_____

_____

_____

Weather expressions

_____

_____

_____

II. Grammar

1. The word *the* is a definite article in English. The singular definite articles in Spanish

   are _____ and _____ , as in _____ **libro** and _____

   carpeta.

2. Most nouns ending with _____ are masculine. Most nouns ending with

   _____ are feminine.

Realidades Ⓐ

Capítulo 1A

Nombre _____

Hora _____

Fecha _____

Practice Workbook **1A–1**

La pregunta perfecta

Complete each sentence using the word or phrase that best describes the picture.

1.  ¿Te gusta _____?

2.  A mí me gusta _____.

3.  ¿Te gusta _____?

4.  No me gusta _____. ¿Y a ti?

5. 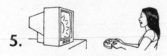 Pues, me gusta mucho _____.

6.  Sí, me gusta mucho _____.

7.  ¿Te gusta mucho _____?

8.  Me gusta _____.

9.  ¡Me gusta mucho _____!

10.  No, ¡no me gusta nada _____!

¿A ti también?

Several friends are talking at the bus stop about what they like and do not like to do. Based on the pictures, write the activity that the first person likes or does not like to do. Then, complete the second person's response. Make sure to use **también** or **tampoco** when expressing agreement and disagreement.

1. ENRIQUE: A mí me gusta mucho _____.
   ¿A ti te gusta?

   DOLORES: Sí, _____.

2. PABLO: Me gusta _____.
   ¿A ti te gusta?

   MARTA: No, _____.

3. JAIME: No me gusta _____.
   ¿A ti te gusta?

   JULIO: No, _____.

4. MARÍA: Me gusta _____.
   ¿A ti te gusta?

   JULIA: No _____.

5. CARMEN: No me gusta nada _____.
   ¿A ti te gusta?

   JOSEFINA: Sí, _____.

6. ROBERTO: Me gusta _____.
   ¿A ti te gusta?

   PEDRO: Sí, _____.

Go Online
PHSchool.com
WEB CODE jcd-0101

Nombre _____

Hora _____

Fecha _____

¿Te gusta o no te gusta?

You are talking to some new students about the things that they like to do. Using the drawings and the model below, complete the following mini-conversations.

Modelo

—¿Te gusta *hablar por teléfono*?

—*Sí, me gusta mucho.*

—¿Te gusta *nadar*?

—*No, no me gusta nada.*

1. —¿Te gusta _____?

_____.

2. —¿Te gusta _____?

_____.

3. —¿Te gusta _____?

_____.

4. —¿Te gusta _____?

_____.

5. —¿Te gusta _____?

_____.

6. —¿Te gusta _____?

_____.

Go Online
PHSchool.com WEB CODE jcd-0102

Realidades A

Capítulo 1A

Nombre _____

Hora _____

Fecha _____

Practice Workbook **1A–4**

¿Qué te gusta hacer?

Complete the dialogues below to find out what activities these friends like and dislike.

1. MIGUEL: ¿Te gusta ir a la escuela?

   RITA: Sí. _____ mucho ir a la escuela.

   ¿Y _____?

   MIGUEL: Sí, a mí me gusta _____ también. No me gusta

   _____ ver la tele _____ jugar videojuegos.

   RITA: _____ tampoco.

2. JUAN: No _____ patinar.

   PAULA: _____ tampoco. Me gusta leer revistas.

   JUAN: ¿_____ más, trabajar o

   _____?

   PAULA: _____ hablar por teléfono.

   JUAN: Sí. A mí _____.

3. AMELIA: A mí _____ pasar tiempo con mis amigos.

   CARLOS: A mí me gusta _____ también.

   AMELIA: ¿Te gusta trabajar?

   CARLOS: No, _____.

   AMELIA: _____ tampoco.

Go Online WEB CODE jcd-0102
PHSchool.com

El infinitivo

Decide what infinitive each picture represents. Then, based on its ending, write the verb in the appropriate column. Use the model as a guide.

	-ar	**-er**	**-ir**
Modelo	_patinar_	_____	_____
1.	_____	_____	_____
2.	_____	_____	_____
3.	_____	_____	_____
4.	_____	_____	_____
5.	_____	_____	_____
6.	_____	_____	_____
7.	_____	_____	_____
8.	_____	_____	_____

Realidades Ⓐ

Capítulo 1A

Nombre _____

Hora _____

Fecha _____

Practice Workbook **1A–6**

Las actividades en común

Cristina is feeling very negative. Using the pictures to help you, write Cristina's negative responses to Lola's questions. Use the model to help you.

Modelo

LOLA: _¿Te gusta patinar?_

CRISTINA: _No, no me gusta nada patinar._

1.

LOLA: _____

CRISTINA: _____

2.

LOLA: _____

CRISTINA: _____

3.

LOLA: _____

CRISTINA: _____

4.

LOLA: _____

CRISTINA: _____

5.

LOLA: _____

CRISTINA: _____

Go Online WEB CODE jcd-0104
PHSchool.com

Realidades Ⓐ

Capítulo 1A

Nombre _____

Fecha _____

Hora _____

Practice Workbook **1A–7**

La conversación completa

At lunch, you overhear a conversation between Sara and Graciela, who are trying to decide what they would like to do after school today. Since it is noisy in the cafeteria, you miss some of what they say. Read the conversation through to get the gist, then fill in the missing lines with what the friends probably said.

GRACIELA: ¿Qué te gusta hacer?

SARA: _____ .

GRACIELA: ¿Nadar? Pero es el invierno. ¡Hace frío!

SARA: Sí. Pues, también _____ .

GRACIELA: Pero hoy es martes y no hay programas buenos en la tele.

SARA: Pues, ¿qué _____ hacer a ti?

GRACIELA: _____ .

SARA: ¡Uf! Hay un problema. No me gusta ni jugar videojuegos ni usar la computadora.

GRACIELA: Hmm . . . ¿_____ ?

SARA: No, _____ nada patinar.

GRACIELA: ¿Te gusta bailar o cantar?

SARA: No, _____ .

GRACIELA: Pues, ¿qué _____ , Sara?

SARA: _____ hablar por teléfono.

GRACIELA: ¡A mí también! ¿Cuál es tu número de teléfono?

WEB CODE jcd-0105
PHSchool.com

Manos a la obra ⬤ *Gramática* **19**

Repaso

Fill in the crossword puzzle below with the actions indicated by the pictures.

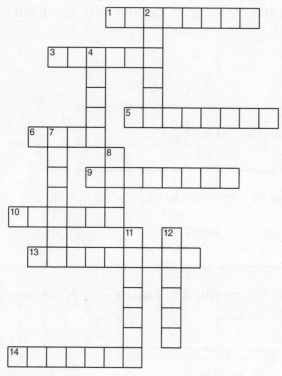

Down ———————————

2.

4.

Across ———————————

1.

3.

5.

6.

9.

10.

13.

14.

7.

8.

11.

12.

Realidades A

Capítulo 1A

Nombre _____

Fecha _____

Hora _____

Practice Workbook **1A–9**

Organizer

I. Vocabulary

Activities I like to do

_____
_____
_____
_____
_____

Activities I may not like to do

_____
_____
_____
_____
_____

Words to say what I like to do

_____
_____
_____

Words to say what I don't like to do

_____
_____
_____

Words to ask what others like to do

_____
_____
_____
_____

II. Grammar

1. The infinitive in English is expressed by writing the word _____ before a verb. In Spanish the infinitive is expressed by the verb endings _____ , _____ , and _____ .

2. In order to say that something doesn't happen in Spanish, use the word _____ before the verb.

3. Use the word _____ to agree with someone who likes something. Use the word _____ to agree with someone who dislikes something.

4. If you do not like either of two choices, use the word _____ .

Realidades Ⓐ

Capítulo 1B

Nombre _____

Fecha _____

Hora _____

Practice Workbook **1B–1**

¿Cómo es?

At school you see many different types of people. Describe each person you see in the picture by writing the appropriate adjective on the corresponding blank.

1. _____

2. _____

3. _____

4. _____

5. _____

6. _____

7. _____

8. _____

Un juego de descripción

Each picture below represents a personality trait. Unscramble the word to identify each trait. Write down the trait, and then circle the picture that corresponds to the unscrambled word.

1.  ísiattcar _____

2.  rvoidate _____

3. 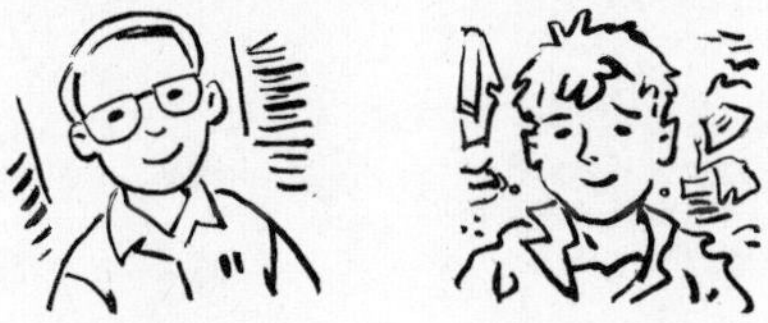 ddonaesdreo _____

4.  jadartobaar _____

5.  iacoarsg _____

6.  zeerosap _____

7. 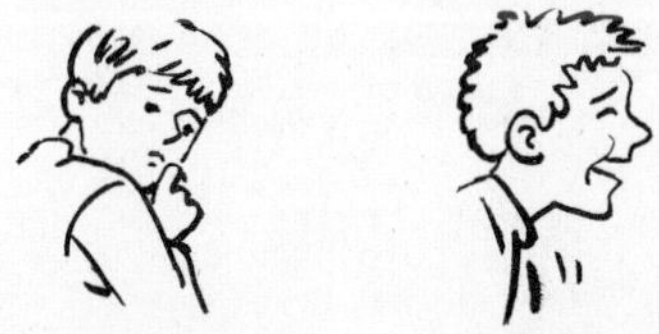 vesrdoaer _____

8.  utoiesdas _____

Realidades Ⓐ

Capítulo 1B

Nombre _____

Fecha _____

Hora _____

Practice Workbook **1B–3**

¿Cómo eres?

Tito is interviewing Jorge and Ana, two new students from Costa Rica. Tito's questions are written below, but most of Jorge's and Ana's answers are missing. Complete their answers, using the model to help you.

Modelo   TITO: Ana, ¿eres perezosa?

ANA: No, *no soy perezosa* _____.

1. TITO: Jorge, ¿eres talentoso?

   JORGE: Sí, _____.

2. TITO: Ana, ¿eres estudiosa?

   ANA: Sí, _____.

3. TITO: Jorge, ¿eres desordenado?

   JORGE: No, _____.

4. TITO: Ana, ¿eres deportista?

   ANA: No, _____.

5. TITO: Jorge, ¿eres sociable?

   JORGE: Sí, _____.

6. TITO: Ana, ¿eres paciente?

   ANA: No, _____.

7. TITO: Jorge, ¿eres inteligente?

   JORGE: Sí, _____.

8. TITO: Ana, ¿eres artística?

   ANA: No, _____.

Go Online WEB CODE jcd-0112
PHSchool.com

Realidades (A)

Capítulo 1B

Nombre _____

Fecha _____

Hora _____

Practice Workbook **1B–4**

¿Qué les gusta?

Based on what each person likes to do, write a description of him or her. Follow the model.

Modelo   A Roberto le gusta esquiar.

Roberto es atrevido.

1. A Esteban le gusta tocar la guitarra.

_____

2. A Pedro le gusta hablar por teléfono.

_____

3. A Claudia le gusta practicar deportes.

_____

4. A Teresa le gusta estudiar.

_____

5. A Luz no le gusta trabajar.

_____

6. A Manuela le gusta ir a la escuela.

_____

7. A Carmen le gusta pasar tiempo con amigos.

_____

8. A Lucía le gusta dibujar.

_____

Realidades Ⓐ

Capítulo 1B

Nombre _____

Fecha _____

Hora _____

Practice Workbook **1B–5**

Me gusta . . .

Some new exchange students at your school are introducing themselves. Using the model as a guide, fill in the blanks in their statements with the actions and adjectives suggested by the pictures. Do not forget to use the correct (masculine or feminine) form of the adjective.

Modelo

A mí _me gusta leer_____.

Yo _soy inteligente_____.

1.

A mí _____.

Yo _____.

2.

A mí _____.

Yo _____.

3.

A mí _____.

Yo _____.

4.

A mí _____.

Yo _____.

5.

A mí _____.

Yo _____.

6.

A mí _____.

Yo _____.

Go Online WEB CODE jcd-0114
PHSchool.com

Realidades A

Capítulo 1B

Nombre _____

Hora _____

Fecha _____

Practice Workbook **1B-6**

¿Un o una?

A. Look at the drawings below and decide if they represent masculine or feminine words. Then, label the item in the space provided. Don't forget to use the appropriate indefinite article (**un** or **una**).

Modelo _____ *un profesor* _____

1. _____

2. _____

3. _____

4. _____

5. _____

6. _____

B. Now, look at the drawings below and describe each person. Make sure to use all the words from the word bank. Don't forget to use the correct definite article (**el** or **la**) and to make the adjectives agree with the nouns.

estudiante	familia	chico	chica	profesor	profesora

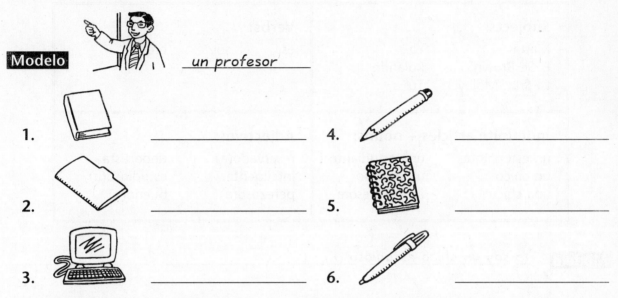

Modelo *La estudiante*

es trabajadora.

1. _____

2. _____

3. _____

4. _____

5. _____

6. _____

Go Online
PHSchool.com
WEB CODE
jcd-0113

Realidades A

Capítulo 1B

Nombre _____

Hora _____

Fecha _____

Practice Workbook **1B–7**

Oraciones completas

Choose sentence parts from each of the word banks below, then put them in the correct order to form complete sentences. Follow the model.

Subjects:		**Verbs:**		
Marta	Yo	es	soy	eres
El Sr. Brown	Rolando			
La Srta. Moloy	Tú			

Indefinite articles + nouns:		**Adjectives:**	
un estudiante	una estudiante	reservado(a)	deportista
un chico	un profesor	inteligente	estudioso(a)
una chica	una profesora	perezoso(a)	bueno(a)

Modelo *Yo soy un chico estudioso.* _____

1. _____

2. _____

3. _____

4. _____

5. _____

6. _____

7. _____

8. _____

9. _____

10. _____

Go Online WEB CODE jcd-0115
PHSchool.com

Realidades Ⓐ

Capítulo 1B

Nombre _____

Fecha _____

Hora _____

Practice Workbook **1B–8**

Repaso

Down

1. según mi ____

2. no paciente

3. no ordenado

5. Un chico/una chica que practica deportes es ____.

6. *I like:* "Me ____."

8.

11. No es trabajador.
Es ____.

13.

15.

16. Le gusta pasar tiempo con amigos. Es ____.

18. —¿Cómo ____?
—Soy sociable.

Across

4.

7. *nice, friendly*

9. no es malo, es ____

10. ¿ ____ se llama?

12.

14.

17.

19.

20.

Repaso del capítulo ━ *Crucigrama* **29**

Realidades Ⓐ

Capítulo 1B

Nombre _____

Fecha _____

Hora _____

Practice Workbook **1B-9**

Organizer

I. Vocabulary

Words that describe me

_____

_____

_____

_____

_____

Words that may describe others

_____

_____

_____

_____

_____

Words to ask what someone is like

_____

_____

_____

Words to tell what I am like

_____

_____

_____

II. Grammar

1. Most feminine adjectives end with the letter _____. Most masculine adjectives end with the letter _____.

2. Adjectives that can be either masculine or feminine may end with the letters _____ (as in the word _____) or the letter _____ (as in the word _____).

3. The two singular definite articles are _____ and _____. The two singular indefinite articles are _____ and _____.

4. In Spanish, adjectives come (before/after) the nouns they describe.

Go Online WEB CODE jcd-0117
PHSchool.com

Realidades

Nombre _____

Hora _____

Capítulo 2A

Fecha _____

Practice Workbook **2A–1**

Las clases

A. Write the name of the item, and the school subject for which you might use it, in the appropriate column below.

¿Qué es?		¿Para qué clase?
1. _____	ESPAÑOL	1. _____
2. _____		2. _____
3. _____	ENGLISH LITERATURE	3. _____
4. _____		4. _____
5. _____	Diccionario Español/Inglés Inglés/Español	5. _____
6. _____	Social Studies	6. _____

B. Now, unscramble the letters in each word below to find out what classes you have today and what you need to bring to school.

1. éilsgn: la clase de _____

2. trea: la clase de _____

3. ncoridcoiia: el _____

4. zlpiá: el _____

5. aduclcralao: la _____

6. ngtíalceoo: la clase de _____

7. birol: el _____

8. lpsñoea: la clase de _____

9. cámtmeistaa: la clase de _____

10. rteaa: la _____

Realidades

Capítulo 2A

Nombre _____

Hora _____

Fecha _____

Practice Workbook **2A–2**

El horario

You have just received your class schedule. Using the model as a guide, write sentences to describe which classes you have and when you have them.

Horario

Hora	Clase
1	inglés
2	matemáticas
3	arte
4	ciencias sociales
5	el almuerzo
6	tecnología
7	español
8	educación física
9	ciencias naturales

Modelo Tengo _la clase de inglés_ en _la primera hora_.

1. Tengo _____ en _____.

2. Tengo _____ en _____.

3. Tengo _____ en _____.

4. Tengo _____ en _____.

5. Tengo _____ en _____.

6. Tengo _____ en _____.

7. Tengo _____ en _____.

8. Tengo _____ en _____.

32 *A primera vista* ▬ *Vocabulario y gramática en contexto*

¿Cómo son las clases?

Your friend Marcos is curious about which classes you like and which ones you don't like. Answer his questions using adjectives that you have learned in this chapter. Follow the model.

Modelo ¿Te gusta la clase de matemáticas?

Sí, _es interesante_____.

1. —¿Te gusta la clase de tecnología?

   —Sí, _____.

2. —¿Te gusta la clase de español?

   —Sí, _____.

3. —¿Te gusta la clase de matemáticas?

   —No, _____.

4. —¿Te gusta la clase de ciencias sociales?

   —Sí, _____.

5. —¿Te gusta la clase de ciencias naturales?

   —No, _____.

6. —¿Te gusta la clase de educación física?

   —No, _____.

7. —¿Te gusta la clase de inglés?

   —Sí, _____.

8. —¿Te gusta la clase de arte?

   —Sí, _____.

Realidades

Nombre _____

Hora _____

Capítulo 2A

Fecha _____

Practice Workbook **2A–4**

¿Qué necesitas?

You are getting ready for school, and your mother wants to make sure you have everything. Answer her questions according to the model.

Modelo   MAMÁ: ¿Tienes la tarea?

TÚ: Sí, _tengo la tarea_ .

1. MAMÁ: ¿Tienes un libro?

   TÚ: Sí, _____.

2. MAMÁ: ¿Necesitas una calculadora?

   TÚ: No, _____.

3. MAMÁ: ¿Tienes una carpeta de argollas para la clase de matemáticas?

   TÚ: No, _____.

4. MAMÁ: ¿Necesitas un diccionario para la clase de español?

   TÚ: Sí, _____.

5. MAMÁ: ¿Tienes el cuaderno para la clase de arte?

   TÚ: No, _____.

6. MAMÁ: ¿Tienes un lápiz?

   TÚ: Sí, _____.

7. MAMÁ: ¿Necesitas el horario?

   TÚ: No, _____.

8. MAMÁ: ¿Tienes un bolígrafo?

   TÚ: Sí, _____.

Go Online   WEB CODE jcd-0202
PHSchool.com

Realidades

Nombre _____

Hora _____

Capítulo 2A

Fecha _____

Practice Workbook **2A–5**

¡Todo el mundo!

A. How would you talk *about* the following people? Write the correct subject pronoun next to their names. Follow the model.

Modelo   Marisol _____ *ella* _____

1. Pablo _____

2. María y Ester _____

3. Marta y yo _____

4. Tú y Marisol _____

5. El doctor Smith _____

6. Jorge y Tomás _____

7. Carmen _____

8. Alicia y Roberto _____

9. Rolando y Elena _____

B. How would you talk *to* the following people? Write the correct subject pronoun next to their names. Follow the model.

Modelo   Tu amiga Josefina _____ *tú* _____

1. El profesor Santiago _____

2. Marta y Carmen _____

3. Anita y yo _____

4. Tu amigo Federico _____

5. La señorita Ibáñez _____

6. Ricardo _____

7. La profesora Álvarez _____

El verbo exacto

A. Fill in the chart below with all the forms of the verbs given.

	yo	tú	él/ella/ Ud.	nosotros/ nosotras	vosotros/ vosotras	ellos/ ellas/Uds.
hablar	hablo				habláis	hablan
estudiar				estudiamos	estudiáis	
enseñar		enseñas			enseñáis	
usar					usáis	
necesitar			necesita		necesitáis	

B. Now, fill in the blanks in the following sentences with the correct forms of the verbs in parentheses.

1. Ella _____ inglés. (estudiar)

2. Yo _____ mucho. (bailar)

3. Nosotros _____ por teléfono. (hablar)

4. Ellos _____ la computadora durante la primera hora. (usar)

5. ¿Quién _____ un bolígrafo? (necesitar)

6. Tú _____ en bicicleta mucho, ¿no? (montar)

7. Uds. _____ muy bien en la clase de arte. (dibujar)

8. Nosotras _____ hoy, ¿no? (patinar)

9. El profesor _____ la lección. (enseñar)

10. Ana y María _____ el libro de español. (necesitar)

11. Jaime _____ todos los días. (caminar)

12. Dolores y yo _____. (bailar)

13. Tú y tus amigos _____ muy bien. (cantar)

Realidades

Nombre _____

Hora _____

Capítulo 2A

Fecha _____

Practice Workbook **2A–7**

¿Qué hacen hoy?

A. Today everyone is doing what he or she likes to do. Follow the model to complete sentences about what everyone is doing.

Modelo   A Luisa le gusta bailar. Hoy _____*ella baila*_____.

1. A ti te gusta cantar. Hoy _____.

2. A mí me gusta hablar por teléfono. Hoy _____.

3. A Francisco le gusta patinar. Hoy _____.

4. A Ud. le gusta dibujar. Hoy _____.

5. A Teresa le gusta practicar deportes. Hoy _____.

B. Using the pictures to help you, tell what everyone is doing today. Follow the model.

   Manuel y Carlos

Modelo   Hoy _____*ellos montan en monopatín*_____.

   Amelia y yo

1.   Hoy _____.

   tú y Roberto

2.   Hoy _____.

   Cristina, Miguel y Linda

3.   Hoy _____.

   tú y yo

4.   Hoy _____.

   Joaquín y Jaime

5.   Hoy _____.

   Sofía y Tomás

6.   Hoy _____.

Go Online
PHSchool.com   WEB CODE jcd-0205

Manos a la obra — *Gramática*   **37**

Realidades

Capítulo 2A

Nombre _____

Hora _____

Fecha _____

Practice Workbook **2A–8**

Repaso

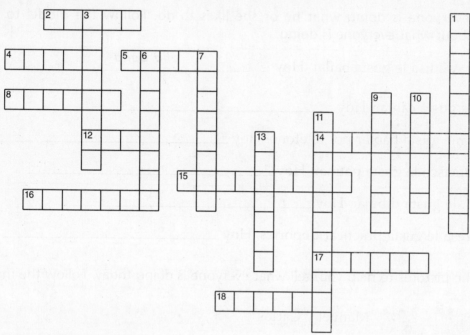

Across

2. No es difícil. Es ____.
4. la ____ de español
5. *homework*
8. educación ____

12. ____ el ____
14. no divertida
15. **ciencias** ____ : *science*
16. ____, octavo, noveno

17. ____ el ____
18. La profesora ____ la clase.

Down

1. ____ la ____
3. ____ **sociales**: *social studies*
6. *lunch*
7. carpeta de ____
9. *schedule*
10. cuarta, ____, sexta

11. ____ la clase de ____
13. primero, segundo, ____

38 *Repaso del capítulo* — *Crucigrama*

Realidades

Capítulo 2A

Nombre _____

Fecha _____

Hora _____

Practice Workbook **2A–9**

Organizer

I. Vocabulary

Classes I take in school

_____

_____

_____

_____

_____

Words to talk about the order of things

_____

_____

_____

_____

_____

_____

_____

Words used to refer to people

_____

_____

_____

_____

Words to describe my classes

_____

_____

_____

_____

_____

II. Grammar

1. The following are subject pronouns in Spanish: _____, _____,

   _____, _____, _____, _____, _____,

   _____, _____, _____, _____, _____

2. Use _____ to address someone formally. Use _____
   to address someone informally.

3. The **-ar** verb endings are: _____ _____ _____ _____ _____ _____

   Now conjugate the verb **hablar**: _____ _____

   _____ _____

   _____ _____

Realidades Ⓐ

Capítulo 2B

Nombre _____

Fecha _____

Hora _____

Practice Workbook **2B–1**

En la clase

Label the items in this Spanish class. Make sure to use the correct definite article (**el** or **la**).

1. _____

2. _____   6. _____   10. _____

3. _____   7. _____   11. _____

4. _____   8. _____   12. _____

5. _____   9. _____   13. _____

Go Online WEB CODE jcd-0211
PHSchool.com

Realidades (A)

Capítulo 2B

Nombre _____

Hora _____

Fecha _____

Practice Workbook **2B–2**

¡Mucha confusión!

You come home after school to find a scene of great confusion in your kitchen. Look at the picture, then describe what you see by filling in the blanks in the sentences below with the appropriate words to indicate location.

1. Paquito está _____ del escritorio.

2. Mamá está _____ de la luz (*the light*).

3. Papá está _____ de la ventana.

4. La papelera está _____ de la puerta.

5. Las hojas de papel están _____ de la mesa.

6. Carmen está _____ de la silla.

7. El reloj está _____ de la mesa.

8. El libro está _____ de la silla.

9. El teclado está _____ de la pantalla.

Realidades A

Capítulo 2B

Nombre _____

Hora _____

Fecha _____

Practice Workbook **2B–3**

¿Dónde está?

Rosario is describing the room where she studies to a friend of hers on the phone. Using the picture below, write what she might say about where each item is located. There may be more than one right answer. Follow the model.

Modelo   La mochila está ___encima de la silla___.

1. El escritorio está _____.

2. La computadora está _____.

3. La papelera está _____.

4. Los disquetes están _____.

5. Una bandera de los Estados Unidos está _____.

6. La silla está _____.

7. El sacapuntas está _____.

8. Los libros de español están _____.

Go Online WEB CODE jcd-0212
PHSchool.com

Realidades Ⓐ

Capítulo 2B

Nombre _____

Fecha _____

Hora _____

Practice Workbook **2B–4**

¿Qué es esto?

Complete the following conversations that you overhear in school.

1. **A:** ¿_____ estudiantes hay en la clase?

   B: _____ veintidós estudiantes en la clase.

2. **A:** ¿_____?

   B: Es la mochila.

3. **A:** ¿_____ está la computadora?

   B: Está allí, al lado de las ventanas.

4. **A:** ¿_____ una bandera en la sala de clases?

   B: Sí, la bandera está allí.

5. **A:** ¿Dónde están los estudiantes?

   B: Los estudiantes _____ la clase de inglés.

6. **A:** ¿Dónde está el teclado?

   B: Está delante _____ la pantalla.

7. **A:** ¿Dónde está el diccionario?

   B: _____ está, debajo del escritorio.

8. **A:** ¿Qué hay _____ la mochila?

   B: Hay muchos libros.

Nombre _____ Hora _____

Fecha _____ Practice Workbook **2B–5**

¿Dónde están?

Spanish teachers are conversing in the faculty room. Fill in their conversations using the correct form of the verb **estar**.

1. —¡Buenos días! ¿Cómo _____ Ud., Sra. López?

   —_____ bien, gracias.

2. —¿Dónde _____ Raúl hoy? No _____ en mi clase.

   —¿Raúl? Él _____ en la oficina.

3. —Yo no tengo mis libros. ¿Dónde _____?

   —Sus libros _____ encima de la mesa, profesor Martínez.

4. —¿Cuántos estudiantes _____ aquí?

   —Diecinueve estudiantes _____ aquí. Uno no _____ aquí.

5. —¿Dónde _____ mi diccionario?

   —El diccionario _____ detrás del escritorio.

6. —¿Cómo _____ los estudiantes hoy?

   —Teresa _____ bien. Jorge y Bernardo _____ regulares.

7. —Bien, profesores, ¿_____ nosotros listos (ready)? Todos los estudiantes _____ en la clase.

Go Online WEB CODE jcd-0214
PHSchool.com

Muchas cosas

A. Fill in the chart below with singular and plural, definite and indefinite forms of the words given. The first word has been completed.

Definite		Indefinite	
singular	plural	singular	plural
la silla	las sillas	una silla	unas sillas
		un cuaderno	
			unos disquetes
	las computadoras		
la mochila			
			unos relojes
		una bandera	
la profesora			

B. Now, fill in each sentence below with words from the chart.

1. Pablo, ¿necesitas _____ de los Estados Unidos? Aquí está.

2. Marta, ¿tienes _____? ¿Qué hora es?

3. Hay _____ Macintosh en la sala de clases.

4. _____ está en la sala de clases. Ella enseña la clase

   de tecnología.

5. Necesito _____ buena. Tengo muchos libros.

WEB CODE jcd-0213
PHSchool.com

Manos a la obra ➖ *Gramática*   **45**

¡Aquí está!

It was a very busy afternoon in your classroom, and things got a little out of order. Write eight sentences describing where things are to help your teacher find everything.

Modelo	*El escritorio está debajo de la computadora* .

1. _____

2. _____

3. _____

4. _____

5. _____

6. _____

7. _____

8. _____

Go Online WEB CODE jcd-0215
PHSchool.com

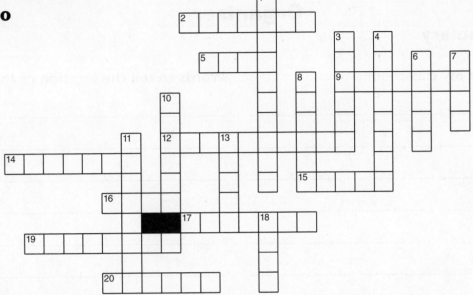

Realidades A

Capítulo 2B

Nombre _____

Fecha _____

Hora _____

Practice Workbook **2B–8**

Repaso

Across

2.

5. la ___ de clases

9.

12.

14.

15. La ___ está detrás del pupitre.

16. La computadora está en la ___ .

17. *window*

19. *diskette*

20.

Down

1. *pencil sharpener*

3. no está encima de, está ___ de

4.

6.

7. al ___ de: *next to*

8. no delante

10.

11.

13. *mouse*

18. No estás aquí, estás ___ .

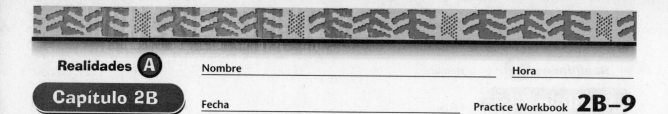

Realidades (A)

Capítulo 2B

Nombre _____

Hora _____

Fecha _____

Practice Workbook **2B-9**

Organizer

I. Vocabulary

Items in my classroom

_____

_____

_____

_____

_____

_____

_____

_____

_____

_____

_____

Words to tell the location of things

_____

_____

_____

_____

_____

_____

_____

_____

II. Grammar

1. The forms of **estar** are: _____ _____

   _____ _____

   _____ _____

2. _____ and _____ are the singular definite articles in

   Spanish. Their plurals are _____ and _____ .

3. The singular indefinite articles are _____ and _____ in

   Spanish. Their plurals are _____ and _____ .

Go Online WEB CODE jcd-0216
PHSchool.com

Realidades Ⓐ
Capítulo 3A

Nombre _____

Fecha _____

Hora _____

Practice Workbook **3A–1**

Tus comidas favoritas

You are getting ready to travel as an exchange student to Spain and you are e-mailing your host family your opinions on different foods. Circle the name of the food item that best completes each sentence below.

1. En el desayuno, yo como ____

    a. cereal.   **b.** un sándwich.

2. Mi comida favorita es ____

    a. el té.   **b.** la pizza.

3. Mi fruta favorita es ____

    a. la fresa.   **b.** la sopa.

4. Para beber, yo prefiero ____

    a. los huevos.   **b.** los refrescos.

5. A mí me gusta el jugo de ____

    a. manzana.   **b.** salchicha.

6. En el almuerzo, yo como ____

    a. un sándwich.   **b.** cereal.

7. Cuando hace frío, yo bebo ____

    a. té helado.   **b.** té.

8. Un BLT es un sándwich de verduras con ____

    a. jamón.   **b.** tocino.

9. Cuando voy a un partido de béisbol, yo como ____

    a. la sopa.   **b.** un perrito caliente.

10. En un sándwich, prefiero ____

    a. el queso.   **b.** el yogur.

Realidades Ⓐ

Capítulo 3A

Nombre _____

Fecha _____

Hora _____

Practice Workbook **3A–2**

¿Desayuno o almuerzo?

Your aunt owns a restaurant and is making her breakfast and lunch menus for the day. Help her by writing the foods and beverages that you think she should serve for each meal in the right places on the menus. Some words may be used more than once.

Go Online WEB CODE jcd-0301
PHSchool.com

Realidades Ⓐ

Capítulo 3A

Nombre _____

Fecha _____

Hora _____

Practice Workbook **3A–3**

Tus preferencias

You are asking Corazón, an exchange student from Venezuela, about various food items that she likes to eat. Use the pictures to help you complete Corazón's answers. Follow the model.

Modelo

TÚ: ¿Tú comes galletas?

CORAZÓN: No. _Yo como huevos_ .

1.

TÚ: ¿Tú comes salchichas?

CORAZÓN: No. _____ .

2.

TÚ: ¿Te gusta más _____ o _____?

CORAZÓN: _____ el café.

3.

TÚ: ¿Tú bebes mucha limonada?

CORAZÓN: No. _____ .

4.

TÚ: ¿Tú comes mucha sopa de verduras?

CORAZÓN: No. _____ .

5.

TÚ: ¿Tú bebes té helado?

CORAZÓN: No. _____ .

6.

TÚ: ¿Tú compartes el desayuno con amigos?

CORAZÓN: No. _____ .

Realidades Ⓐ

Capítulo 3A

Nombre _____

Fecha _____

Hora _____

Practice Workbook **3A–4**

¿Qué comes?

Carolina, the new exchange student, is having a hard time figuring out the kinds of foods that people like to eat. Answer her questions in complete sentences, using **¡Qué asco!** and **¡Por supuesto!** in at least one answer each.

1. ¿Comes hamburguesas con plátanos?

_____

2. ¿Comes el sándwich de jamón y queso en el almuerzo?

_____

3. ¿Bebes leche en el desayuno?

_____

4. ¿Te gusta la pizza con la ensalada de frutas?

_____

5. ¿Comes papas fritas en el desayuno?

_____

6. ¿Compartes la comida con tu familia?

_____

7. ¿Comes un perro caliente todos los días?

_____

8. ¿Te encantan las galletas con leche?

_____

Go Online WEB CODE jcd-0302
PHSchool.com

Realidades A

Capítulo 3A

Nombre _____

Fecha _____

Hora _____

Practice Workbook **3A–5**

El verbo correcto

A. Fill in the chart below with all the forms of the verbs given.

	yo	tú	él/ella/Ud.	nosotros/ nosotras	vosotros/ vosotras	ellos/ ellas/Uds.
comer			come		coméis	
beber		bebes			bebéis	
comprender	comprendo				comprendéis	
escribir				escribimos	escribís	
compartir					compartís	comparten

B. Now, using the verbs from Part A, write the missing verb to complete each sentence below.

1. Antonio _____ sus papas fritas con Amelia.

2. Uds. _____ los sándwiches de queso.

3. Yo _____ las salchichas en el desayuno.

4. Nosotros _____ el té helado.

5. Ana _____ la tarea.

6. Tú _____ una carta al profesor.

7. Yo _____ el pan con Jorge.

8. Él _____ jugo de naranja en el desayuno.

9. Nosotros _____ con un lápiz.

10. Paula y Guillermo hablan y _____ español.

11. ¿_____ tú leche en el desayuno?

12. Manolo y Federico _____ las galletas con Susana.

Realidades A

Capítulo 3A

Nombre _____

Fecha _____

Hora _____

Practice Workbook **3A-6**

¿Qué te gusta?

A. List your food preferences in the blanks below.

Me gusta	Me gustan	Me encanta	Me encantan
_____	_____	_____	*los sándwiches*
_____	_____	_____	_____
			_____

B. Now, organize your preferences into complete sentences. Follow the model.

Modelo *Me encantan los sándwiches.* _____

1. _____

2. _____

3. _____

4. _____

5. _____

6. _____

7. _____

8. _____

C. Using the words given, write a sentence about each food. Follow the model.

Modelo El té (encantar) *Me encanta el té* . _____

1. los plátanos (gustar) _____

2. la pizza (encantar) _____

3. las papas fritas (encantar) _____

4. el pan (gustar) _____

Go Online WEB CODE jcd-0304
PHSchool.com

Mini-conversaciones

Fill in the blanks in the mini-conversations below with the most logical question or answer.

1. —¿Comparten Uds. el sándwich de jamón y queso?

—Sí, nosotros _____ el sándwich.

2. —¿_____ tú todos los días?

—No, nunca corro. No me gusta.

3. —¿_____ en el desayuno?

—¡Qué asco! No me gustan los plátanos.

4. —¿_____?

—Sí, profesora. Comprendemos la lección.

5. —¿_____?

—Mi jugo favorito es el jugo de manzana.

6. —¿_____?

—Más o menos. Me gusta más la pizza.

7. —¿_____?

—¡Por supuesto! Me encanta el cereal.

Realidades Ⓐ

Capítulo 3A

Nombre _____

Hora _____

Fecha _____

Practice Workbook **3A-8**

Repaso

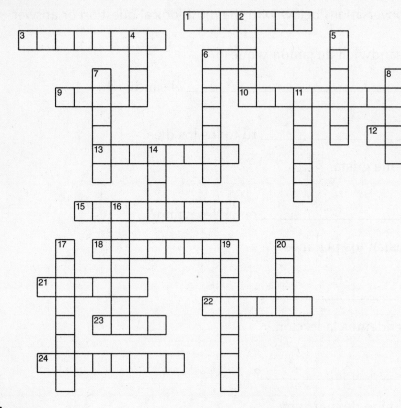

Down

2. más o ___

4. ¡Qué ___! No me gustan los guisantes.

5.

6.

7. el té ___

8. las ___ fritas

11. *food*

14.

16. un jugo de ___

17. No como carne. Me gusta la sopa de ___.

19. En los Estados Unidos el ___ es un sándwich y algo de beber.

20. un ___ de naranja

Across

1. *always*

3. El Monstruo Comegalletas come muchas ___.

6. el ___ tostado

9. Me gusta el sándwich de jamón y ___.

10.

12.

13. Muchas personas comen cereales con leche en el ___.

15. ¿Te gusta ___ el almuerzo con tus amigos?

18. Me gusta la ___ de frutas, no de lechuga.

21. un yogur de ___

22.

23.

24. el perrito ___

Realidades **A**

Capítulo 3A

Nombre _____

Hora _____

Fecha _____

Practice Workbook **3A–9**

Organizer

I. Vocabulary

Breakfast foods

_____

_____

_____

_____

_____

Lunch foods

_____

_____

_____

_____

_____

Beverages

_____

_____

_____

_____

Words to express likes/dislikes

_____

_____

_____

_____

II. Grammar

1. The **-er** verb endings are: -_____   -_____

    -_____   -_____

    -_____   -_____

    Now conjugate the verb **beber**:   _____   _____

    _____   _____

    _____   _____

2. The **-ir** verb endings are: -_____   -_____

    -_____   -_____

    -_____   -_____

    Now conjugate the verb **compartir**:   _____   _____

    _____   _____

    _____   _____

3. To use **me gusta** and **me encanta** to talk about plural nouns, you add the letter _____ to the end of the verb.

¡A cenar!

A. You are having a party, and you need to make a shopping list. Write at least three items that you might want to buy under each category. You may use vocabulary from other chapters.

La ensalada de frutas:

_____

_____

_____

_____

_____

Las verduras:

_____

_____

_____

_____

_____

La carne:

_____

_____

_____

_____

_____

Bebemos:

_____

_____

_____

_____

_____

B. Now write three things your guests might like to eat after dinner.

_____

_____

_____

Más comida

A. Name the most logical food category to which each group of items belongs.

1. el bistec, el pollo, el pescado _____

2. las zanahorias, la cebolla, los guisantes _____

3. las uvas, las manzanas _____

4. el postre, la mantequilla _____

B. Now, answer the following questions logically in complete sentences.

1. ¿Debemos comer las uvas, el helado o los pasteles para mantener la salud?

   _____

2. ¿Es sabrosa la ensalada de frutas con las papas o con los plátanos?

   _____

3. ¿Comemos la mantequilla con el pan tostado o con el bistec?

   _____

4. ¿Bebemos los refrescos o el agua para mantener la salud?

   _____

C. Using the foods below, write sentences telling whether we should or shouldn't eat or drink each thing to maintain good health. Follow the model.

Modelo   el agua *Debemos beber el agua para mantener la salud.*

1. los tomates _____

2. las grasas _____

3. los plátanos _____

4. las uvas _____

5. la mantequilla _____

6. la leche _____

La respuesta perfecta

You are learning about fitness and nutrition at school, and your friends want to know more. Answer their questions or respond to their statements in complete sentences.

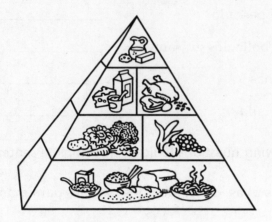

1. ¿Es el tomate bueno para la salud?

   _____

2. ¿Por qué caminas todos los días?

   _____

3. ¿La mantequilla es buena para la salud?

   _____

4. Creo que las grasas son horribles.

   _____

5. ¿Qué debes hacer para mantener la salud?

   _____

6. ¿Prefieres levantar pesas o caminar?

   _____

7. Creo que los espaguetis son sabrosos. ¿Y tú?

   _____

Go Online WEB CODE jcd-0312
PHSchool.com

Realidades Ⓐ

Capítulo 3B

Nombre _____

Hora _____

Fecha _____

Practice Workbook **3B–4**

¿Qué comes?

Angel is asking his friend Estela about foods she likes. Fill in the blanks with the foods suggested by the pictures, then complete Estela's answers.

1. —¿Te gustan _____?

   —No, _____.

2. —¿Prefieres _____ con _____ en el almuerzo o en la cena?

   —_____ en el almuerzo.

3. —¿Te gustan _____?

   —Sí, _____.

4. —¿Prefieres _____ de chocolate o de fruta?

   —_____ de chocolate·

5. —¿Comes _____?

   —Sí, _____.

6. —¿Siempre comes _____ en el almuerzo?

   —No, _____.

7. —¿Te gusta el _____ con _____?

   —Sí, _____.

Realidades (A)

Capítulo 3B

Nombre _____

Fecha _____

Hora _____

Practice Workbook **3B–5**

Las descripciones

A. Fill in the chart below with the singular and plural, masculine and feminine forms of the adjectives given.

Masculine		Feminine	
singular	plural	singular	plural
sabroso			
	prácticos		
		fácil	
	aburridos		
			difíciles
divertido			
		artística	
			buenas
trabajador			

B. Now, complete the sentences below, using some of the words from the chart above. There may be more than one right answer.

1. La ensalada de frutas es _____ para la salud.

2. Me gustan mis clases; son _____ .

3. La tarea de matemáticas es _____ .

4. Te gustan las computadoras porque son _____ .

5. Mi profesor no come pescado porque cree que no es _____ .

6. Mis amigos son _____ ; dibujan muy bien.

7. Tus amigos son muy _____ ; trabajan mucho.

8. Esquiar y nadar son actividades muy _____ .

Go Online WEB CODE jcd-0313
PHSchool.com

¿Cómo son?

Describe the following people using the pictures as clues. Use a form of **ser** plus an adjective. Follow the model.

Modelo

¿Cómo _____*es*_____ él?

Él es popular _____.

1.

¿Cómo _____ él?

_____.

2.

¿Cómo _____ ella?

_____.

3.

¿Cómo _____ ellas?

_____.

4.

¿Cómo _____ ellos?

_____.

5.

¿Cómo _____ nosotras?

_____.

6.

¿Cómo _____ yo?

_____.

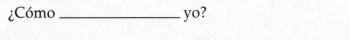

Realidades Ⓐ

Capítulo 3B

Nombre _____

Hora _____

Fecha _____

Practice Workbook **3B–7**

La buena salud

Your cousin Eva has started a new diet and exercise program, and she has sent you an e-mail telling you all about it. Read her e-mail and answer the questions below in complete sentences.

Hola,

Para mantener la salud, como muchas verduras y frutas cada día. ¡Creo que son sabrosas! Yo hago ejercicio también. Me gusta caminar, pero prefiero levantar pesas. Siempre bebo mucha agua, y es mi bebida favorita. No debemos comer los pasteles, porque son malos para la salud. ¿Estás de acuerdo?

---

1. ¿Qué come Eva para mantener la salud?

   _____

2. ¿Eva hace ejercicio?

   _____

3. ¿A Eva le gustan las frutas?

   _____

4. ¿Qué prefiere hacer Eva para mantener la salud?

   _____

5. ¿Cuál es la bebida favorita de Eva?

   _____

6. ¿Por qué no debemos comer los pasteles?

   _____

Go Online WEB CODE jcd-0315
PHSchool.com

Realidades A

Capítulo 3B

Nombre _____

Fecha _____

Hora _____

Practice Workbook **3B–8**

Repaso

Across

3. el ___

5.

6. Prefiero las ensaladas de ___ y tomate.

8. el ___

10. Debes comer bien para mantener la ___.

12. *drinks*

13. el ___

16. *something*

18. Tengo ___. Necesito comer.

20. estoy de ___

22. Los ___ no son buenos para la salud pero son sabrosos.

24. ___ comer bien para mantener la salud.

Down

1. *meat*

2. un ___

4. las ___ verdes

7. los ___

9. Yo prefiero ___ la salud y comer bien.

11. las ___

14. *carrots*

15. Me gusta la comida de tu mamá. Es muy ___.

17.

19.

21. *dinner*

23. ___ los días; siempre

Organizer

I. Vocabulary

Fruits and vegetables

_____

_____

_____

_____

Starches

_____

_____

_____

_____

General food terms

_____

_____

_____

_____

Types of exercise

_____

_____

_____

_____

II. Grammar

1. Adjectives are _____ when describing one person or thing, and
   _____ when describing more than one person or thing.

2. To make an adjective plural, add _____ if the last letter is a vowel
   and _____ if the last letter is a consonant.

3. The forms of **ser** are: _____   _____

   _____   _____

   _____   _____

Go Online WEB CODE jcd-0316
PHSchool.com

¿Qué hacen?

What do the people in your neighborhood like to do in their free time? Complete the following sentences based on the pictures.

1. La Sra. García lee un libro en

_____.

2. Jesús levanta pesas en

_____.

3. Los lunes tengo _____

con el Sr. Casals.

4. A Pedro le gusta pasar tiempo en _____

cuando tiene tiempo libre.

5. Elena y Tomás prefieren ir al _____

los viernes.

6. A mí me gusta ir a _____

cuando hace calor.

7. A Sara le gusta caminar en

_____.

8. Me gusta ir al _____

para comer.

Realidades Ⓐ

Capítulo 4A

Nombre _____

Hora _____

Fecha _____

Practice Workbook **4A–2**

¿Adónde vas?

Where do you go to do the following things? Write your answers in complete sentences. Follow the model.

Modelo esquiar _____*Voy a las montañas para esquiar.*_____

1. trabajar _____

2. leer, estudiar _____

3. hablar español _____

4. correr, caminar _____

5. ir de compras _____

6. tocar el piano _____

7. comer, beber _____

8. ver una película _____

9. nadar _____

10. hacer ejercicio _____

11. estar con amigos _____

12. levantar pesas _____

Go Online WEB CODE jcd-0401
PHSchool.com

Realidades Ⓐ

Capítulo 4A

Nombre _____

Hora _____

Fecha _____

Practice Workbook **4A-3**

¿Qué hacen?

An exchange student from Chile wants to know where people go to do certain activities. Complete each conversation with the verb suggested by the first picture, then answer the questions based on the second illustration.

Modelo

—Cuando __ves__ una película, ¿adónde vas?

—__Voy al cine__ .

1. —Cuando _____, ¿adónde vas?

—_____ .

2. —Cuando _____, ¿adónde vas?

—_____ .

3. —Cuando _____, ¿adónde vas?

—_____ .

4. —Cuando _____, ¿adónde vas?

—_____ .

5. —Cuando _____, ¿adónde vas?

—_____ .

6. —Cuando _____, ¿adónde vas?

—_____ .

Realidades **A**

Capítulo 4A

Nombre _____

Fecha _____

Hora _____

Practice Workbook **4A–4**

El horario de Tito

Look at Tito's schedule for part of the month of February. Then answer the questions about his activities in complete sentences.

lunes	martes	miércoles	jueves	viernes	sábado	domingo
F E B R E R O						
8 trabajar	**9** nadar	**10** estudiar en la biblioteca	**11** trabajar	**12** ir al cine	**13** ir al gimnasio	**14** ir a la iglesia
15 trabajar	**16** practicar karate	**17** estudiar en la biblioteca	**18** trabajar	**19** ir al cine	**20** ir al gimnasio	**21** ir a la iglesia
22 trabajar	**23** levantar pesas	**24** estudiar en la biblioteca	**25** trabajar	**26** ir al cine	**27** ir al gimnasio	**28** ir a la iglesia

1. ¿Qué hace Tito los viernes?

_____

2. ¿Cuándo estudia Tito en la biblioteca?

_____

3. ¿Cuándo hace ejercicio Tito?

_____

4. Generalmente, ¿cuándo trabaja Tito?

_____

5. ¿Qué hace Tito los lunes?

_____

6. ¿Cuándo va a la iglesia Tito?

_____

7. ¿Qué hace Tito los fines de semana?

_____

Go Online WEB CODE jcd-0402
PHSchool.com

Realidades Ⓐ

Capítulo 4A

Nombre _____

Fecha _____

Hora _____

Practice Workbook **4A–5**

Las actividades favoritas

Students are making plans for what they will do after school. Complete their conversations with the correct forms of the verb **ir**.

1. LOLIS: Hoy, (yo) _____ al parque después de las clases.

    ELIA: ¡Qué bien! María y yo _____ al cine.

    LOLIS: Mi amigo Pablo también _____ al cine hoy.

2. MARTA: Hola, Juan. ¿Adónde _____?

    JUAN: Pues, _____ a la clase de inglés, pero después

              _____ al centro comercial. ¿Y tú?

    MARTA: Pues, mis padres _____ a la playa y yo

              _____ con ellos.

    JUAN: ¡Qué bueno! ¿Cuándo _____ Uds.?

    MARTA: Nosotros _____ después de las clases.

3. RODOLFO: ¡Hola, Pablo, Felipe!

    PABLO Y FELIPE: ¡Hola, Rodolfo!

    RODOLFO: ¿Adónde _____ Uds.?

    PABLO: Pues, yo _____ a casa con unos amigos.

    FELIPE: Yo no _____ con él. _____ a la mezquita.

              ¿Y tú?

    RODOLFO: Catrina y yo _____ a la piscina. Ella _____

              al gimnasio más tarde.

    PABLO: Mi amiga Elena _____ al gimnasio con ella. Creo que

              ellas _____ a las cinco.

    FELIPE: Es muy tarde. Tengo que _____. ¡Hasta luego!

La pregunta perfecta

A. Complete the following questions with the correct question words.

1. ¿_____ es el chico más alto de la clase?

2. ¿_____ vas al cine? ¿Hoy?

3. ¿_____ es tu número de teléfono?

4. ¿_____ te llamas?

5. ¿_____ vas después de las clases hoy?

6. ¿_____ está mi libro de español?

7. ¿_____ es esto?

8. ¿_____ años tienes?

B. Now, form your own questions using some of the question words above.

1. ¿_____?

2. ¿_____?

3. ¿_____?

4. ¿_____?

5. ¿_____?

6. ¿_____?

7. ¿_____?

Go Online WEB CODE jcd-0404
PHSchool.com

Realidades Ⓐ

Capítulo 4A

Nombre _____

Fecha _____

Hora _____

Practice Workbook **4A–7**

¿Qué haces?

You are talking with your parents about your plans for the evening. They have lots of questions. Your answers are given below. Write your parents' questions in the spaces provided.

TUS PADRES: ¿_____?

TÚ: Voy a un restaurante.

TUS PADRES: ¿_____?

TÚ: Voy con unos amigos.

TUS PADRES: ¿_____?

TÚ: Ellos se llaman Roberto y Ana.

TUS PADRES: ¿_____?

TÚ: Roberto y Ana son de México.

TUS PADRES: ¿_____?

TÚ: Pues, Roberto es inteligente, trabajador y paciente.

TUS PADRES: ¿_____?

TÚ: Ana es deportista y estudiosa.

TUS PADRES: ¿_____?

TÚ: Después, nosotros vamos al cine.

TUS PADRES: ¿_____?

TÚ: ¿Después? Pues, voy a casa. ¡Uds. hacen muchas preguntas!

Realidades Ⓐ

Capítulo 4A

Nombre _____

Fecha _____

Hora _____

Practice Workbook **4A–8**

Repaso

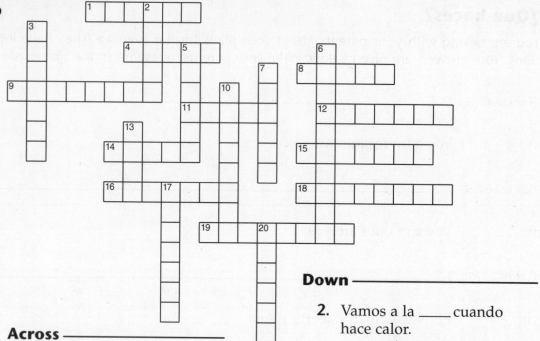

Across

1. *temple*

4.

8. ¡No me ____!

9. *mosque*

11. –¿Con ____ vas al cine?
    – Con Ana.

12. Tengo que ir a la ____ de piano.

14. No tengo tiempo ____.

15. Para la Navidad todos van de ____.

16. *after*

18. Me gusta la ____ *Desperado*.

19.

Down

2. Vamos a la ____ cuando hace calor.

3.

5. Me gusta caminar en el ____.

6.

7. el ____ comercial

10. Voy al ____ para levantar pesas.

13. Vamos al ____ para ver una película.

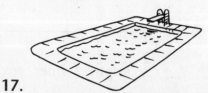

17.

20. Vas al ____ para trabajar.

Realidades **A**

Capítulo 4A

Nombre _____

Fecha _____

Hora _____

Practice Workbook **4A–9**

Organizer

I. Vocabulary

Some of my favorite places

_____

_____

_____

_____

_____

_____

Words to talk about other places

_____

_____

_____

_____

_____

_____

Interrogative words

_____

_____

_____

_____

_____

_____

Phrases related to leisure activities

_____

_____

_____

_____

II. Grammar

1. The forms of the verb **ir** are: _____ _____

   _____ _____

   _____ _____

2. **A.** In order to get information in English, we use the words *who, what, where, when, why,* and *how*. In Spanish these words are: _____ , _____ ,

   _____ , _____ , _____ y _____ .

   B. When asking a question in Spanish, the verb comes _____ the subject.

Realidades Ⓐ

Capítulo 4B

Nombre _____

Fecha _____

Hora _____

Practice Workbook **4B–1**

¿Eres deportista?

Write the name of the sport or activity indicated by the art.

1. _____

2. _____

3. _____

4. _____

5. _____

6. _____

7. _____

8. _____

9. _____

Go Online WEB CODE jcd-0411
PHSchool.com

Las invitaciones

You and your friends are making plans for the weekend. Complete your friends' invitations with the activities suggested by the pictures. Then accept the offers using complete sentences. Follow the model.

Modelo

—¿Te gustaría _____*ir al cine*_____ este fin de semana?

— ___*Sí, me gustaría ir al cine*___ .

1. —¿Puedes _____ este fin de semana?

— _____ .

2. —¿Quieres _____ este fin de semana?

— _____ .

3. —¿Puedes _____ este fin de semana?

— _____ .

4. —¿Te gustaría _____ este fin de semana?

— _____ .

5. —¿Quieres _____ este fin de semana?

— _____ .

Realidades Ⓐ

Capítulo 4B

Nombre _____

Fecha _____

Hora _____

Practice Workbook **4B–3**

¿Cómo están?

You have just arrived at school and are asking how your friends are doing. Using the pictures to help you, fill in the blanks with the correct form of **estar** and the appropriate adjective. Don't forget to make the adjective agree with the subject!

1. —¿Cómo está ella?

   —_____.

2. —¿Cómo está él?

   —_____.

3. —¿Cómo están ellos?

   —_____.

4. —¿Cómo están ellas?

   —_____.

5. —¿Cómo están los estudiantes?

   —_____.

6. —¿Cómo está él?

   —_____.

Go **Online** WEB CODE jcd-0412
PHSchool.com

Realidades Ⓐ

Capítulo 4B

Nombre _____

Hora _____

Fecha _____

Practice Workbook **4B–4**

¿A qué hora?

Lucía is very busy on the weekends. Answer the questions about her schedule using complete sentences.

Modelo   ¿A qué hora usa la computadora?

Usa la computadora a las siete y media de la noche.

1. ¿A qué hora tiene que trabajar Lucía?

_____

2. ¿A qué hora va a casa?

_____

3. ¿Qué hacen Lucía y su amiga a las ocho de la mañana?

_____

4. ¿A qué hora come la cena Lucía?

_____

5. ¿Cuándo estudian ella y su amigo?

_____

6. ¿Adónde va Lucía esta noche? ¿A qué hora?

_____

 WEB CODE jcd-0412

Realidades A

Capítulo 4B

Nombre

Hora

Fecha

Practice Workbook **4B–5**

Los planes

It is 10:00 Saturday morning, and you and your friends are making plans for the afternoon and evening. Using a form of **ir** + **a** + *infinitive,* write complete sentences about everyone's plans. Follow the model.

Modelo   María

María va a ir de compras esta tarde .

1.   Ana y yo

_____ .

2.   Pablo

_____ .

3.   Yo

_____ .

4.   Mis amigos

_____ .

5.   Tú

_____ .

6.   Nosotros

_____ .

7.   Ud.

_____ .

8.   Ana y Lorena

_____ .

Go Online WEB CODE jcd-0413
PHSchool.com

Realidades Ⓐ

Capítulo 4B

Nombre _____

Hora _____

Fecha _____

Practice Workbook **4B-6**

Demasiadas preguntas

Your friends are asking you to make plans for this weekend, but you are not able to do anything that they have suggested. Using the pictures to help you, respond to their questions using **ir** + **a** + *infinitive.* Follow the model.

Modelo   ¿Puedes ir al partido mañana?

No, no puedo. Voy a correr mañana.

1. ¿Quieres ir al partido esta noche?

_____.

2. ¿Te gustaría ir al cine conmigo esta noche?

_____.

3. ¿Quieres jugar al golf esta tarde?

_____.

4. ¿Puedes jugar videojuegos conmigo el viernes?

_____.

5. ¿Te gustaría ir de compras mañana por la noche?

_____.

6. ¿Te gustaría ir al baile conmigo esta noche?

_____.

7. ¿Quieres ir a la biblioteca conmigo?

_____.

8. ¿Puedes ir de cámping conmigo este fin de semana?

_____.

Realidades Ⓐ
Capítulo 4B

Nombre _____

Hora _____

Fecha _____

Practice Workbook **4B-7**

¿A qué juegas?

Friends are talking about the sports that they enjoy playing. Write the correct form of the verb **jugar** to complete each sentence.

1. —¿Marta juega al vóleibol?

   —Sí, Rodrigo y ella _____ todos los días.

2. —Oye, ¿puedes jugar al básquetbol con nosotros?

   —Lo siento, pero no _____ bien.

3. —¿A qué juegan Uds.?

   —Nosotros _____ al golf.

4. —Ellas juegan al tenis muy bien, ¿no?

   —Sí, _____ muy bien.

5. —¿_____ Ud. al básquetbol a la una?

   —No. Tengo que ir a un concierto.

6. —Yo juego al fútbol hoy.

   —¡Ay, me encanta el fútbol! ¡_____ contigo!

7. —¿Tú y Manuel jugáis al béisbol esta tarde?

   —Sí. ¡_____ todos los días!

8. —¿Qué hace Luz esta noche?

   —Ella _____ al vóleibol a las ocho.

Go Online WEB CODE jcd-0414
PHSchool.com

Realidades Ⓐ

Capítulo 4B

Nombre _____

Hora _____

Fecha _____

Practice Workbook **4B-8**

Repaso

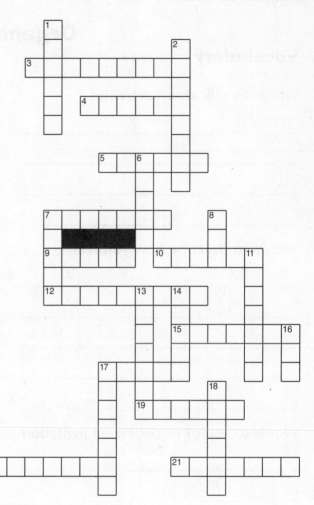

Across

3. No puedo jugar. Estoy ____ ocupado.

4. *sad*

5.

7. Me gusta ver el ____ de béisbol.

9. yo sé, tú ____

10. Lo ____, pero no puedo.

12.  el fútbol ____

15.

17. El *Jitterbug* es un ____.

19. *Great!*

20. Vamos al ____ para escuchar música.

21. *with me*

Down

1. Vamos a la ____ de cumpleaños de Paco.

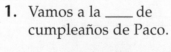

2.

6. *afternoon*; la ____

7. me gusta ir de *fishing*

8. el ____ de semana

11. Ella trabaja mucho, siempre está ____.

13.

14. Es después de la tarde; la ____.

16. *Hey!*

17.

18. Voy a la escuela a las siete de la ____.

Organizer

I. Vocabulary

Words to talk about activities

_____

_____

_____

Words to describe how you feel

_____

_____

_____

Words to accept or decline an invitation

_____

_____

_____

Names of sports

_____

_____

_____

_____

_____

Words to say when something happens

_____

_____

_____

_____

II. Grammar

1. The forms of the verb **jugar** are: _____ _____

   _____ _____

   _____ _____

2. The preposition **con** becomes _____ to mean "with me" and _____ to mean "with you."

3. To say you are going to do something, you use the verb _____ + _____ + the action you are going to perform.

Writing, Audio & Video Activities

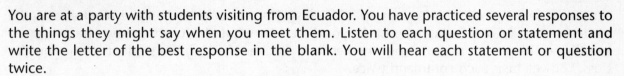

Realidades A

Para empezar

Nombre _____

Fecha _____

Hora _____

AUDIO

Actividad 1

You are at a party with students visiting from Ecuador. You have practiced several responses to the things they might say when you meet them. Listen to each question or statement and write the letter of the best response in the blank. You will hear each statement or question twice.

a.	Me llamo ...	**1.** _____
b.	Muy bien, gracias.	**2.** _____
c.	Regular.	**3.** _____
d.	Mucho gusto.	**4.** _____
e.	Igualmente.	**5.** _____
f.	Hasta mañana.	**6.** _____

Actividad 2

You have lost your dog, so you put up signs in your neighborhood asking your neighbors to call you if they see him. You will hear six messages on your answering machine from neighbors who have seen your dog. You will not understand everything they say, but listen carefully to find out their house number and what time they called so that you can track down your dog. Write down each house number and time on the chart. You will hear each message twice.

	NÚMERO DE CASA (House number)	HORA DE LA LLAMADA (Time of call)
1.	_____	_____
2.	_____	_____
3.	_____	_____
4.	_____	_____
5.	_____	_____
6.	_____	_____

Nombre _____

Hora _____

Fecha _____

AUDIO

Actividad 3

A new student has come into your Spanish class. He seems lost when the teacher asks the students to take out certain items. As you listen to what the teacher says, help him by identifying the picture that matches the item the teacher is asking the students to get out for class. You will hear each command twice.

| Modelo | _f_ | 1. _____ | 2. _____ | 3. _____ | 4. _____ | 5. _____ |

a.

b.

c.

d.

e.

f.

Actividad 4

Your teacher is using a map and an alphabet/number grid to plan a class trip to Spain. The five dots on the grid represent cities in Spain where your group will stop. Listen as you hear the first letter/number combination, as in the game of Bingo. Find that dot on the grid and label it "1." Next to it, write the name of the city. After you hear the second letter/number combination, find the second dot and label it "2," writing the name of the city next to it, and so on for the rest of the dots. Connect the dots to show the route of the class trip. You will hear each phrase twice.

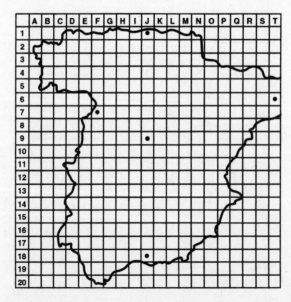

Realidades Ⓐ

Para empezar

Nombre

Fecha

Hora

AUDIO

Actividad 5

While on vacation in Uruguay, your teacher visits an elementary school classroom. Each student in the class tells your teacher his or her birthday (**cumpleaños**) and what the weather is like at that time of the year in Uruguay. Remember, in South America the seasons are the reverse of those in the United States. In the first column write out each student's date of birth, and in the second column what season his or her birthday is in. You will hear each sentence twice.

	DATE OF BIRTH	SEASON
1. Juan	_____	_____
2. María	_____	_____
3. Miguel	_____	_____
4. Óscar	_____	_____
5. Carolina	_____	_____
6. Marta	_____	_____
7. Elena	_____	_____
8. Pedro	_____	_____

Realidades A

Para empezar

Nombre _____

Fecha _____

Hora _____

WRITING

Actividad 6

Describe the monster below, telling how many of each body part he has (**El monstruo tiene ...**). Each blank corresponds to one letter. Each letter corresponds to a number, which appears underneath the blank. Use these numbers to figure out which sentence refers to which body part. The first one has been done for you.

Modelo El monstruo tiene <u>D</u> <u>O</u> <u>S</u>   <u>C</u> <u>A</u> <u>B</u> <u>E</u> <u>Z</u> <u>A</u> <u>S</u>.
                         9 15 20   2 10 19 1 3 10 20

1. El monstruo tiene ___ ___ ___ ___   ___ ___ ___ ___.
                15 2 8 15   15 17 15 20

2. El monstruo tiene ___ ___ ___   ___ ___ ___ ___ ___ en cada cabeza.
                6 22 10   22 10 4 5 3

3. El monstruo tiene ___ ___ ___   ___ ___ ___ ___ en cada cabeza.
                6 22 10   19 15 2 10

4. El monstruo tiene ___ ___ ___ ___ ___ ___   ___ ___ ___ ___ ___ ___.
                2 6 10 11 4 15   19 4 10 3 15 20

5. El monstruo tiene ___ ___ ___ ___   ___ ___ ___ ___ ___ en cada mano.
                11 4 1 20   9 1 9 15 20

6. El monstruo tiene ___ ___ ___ ___   ___ ___ ___ ___ ___ ___ ___.
                20 1 5 20   16 5 1 4 22 10 20

Realidades Ⓐ

Para empezar

Nombre _____

Fecha _____

Hora _____

WRITING

Actividad 7

A. It is September and school is finally in **session. You already have some important dates to** mark on the calendar. To make sure you **have the right day, write the day of the week** that each date falls on.

SEPTIEMBRE						
lunes	martes	miércoles	jueves	viernes	sábado	domingo
		1	2	3	4	5
6	7	8	9	10	11	12
13	14	15	16	17	18	19
20	21	22	23	24	25	26
27	28	29	30			

1. el tres de septiembre _____

2. el veinte de septiembre _____

3. el primero de septiembre _____

4. el veinticuatro de septiembre _____

5. el doce de septiembre _____

6. el dieciocho de septiembre _____

7. el siete de septiembre _____

B. Now, write in what month the following **holidays occur.**

1. el Día de San Valentín _____

2. el Día de San Patricio _____

3. la Navidad _____

4. el Año Nuevo _____

5. el Día de la Independencia _____

Realidades (A)

Para empezar

Nombre _____

Fecha _____

Hora _____

WRITING

Actividad 8

Answer the questions below according to the map.

1. ¿Qué tiempo hace en el norte de México?

   _____

2. ¿Hace buen tiempo en el sur?

   _____

3. ¿Qué tiempo hace en el centro de México?

   _____

4. ¿Hace frío o calor en el oeste?

   _____

5. ¿Qué tiempo hace en el este?

   _____

6. ¿Qué estación es, probablemente?

   _____

Nombre _____

Hora _____

Fecha _____

VIDEO

Introducción

Actividad 1

Do you like the video so far? Did you enjoy meeting the characters? Are you curious to find out more about their home cities? Look at the map below. Then, write the names of the video friends that live at each location. As you are doing this exercise, begin to familiarize yourself with the names of these locations: Madrid, España; Ciudad de México, México; San José, Costa Rica; San Antonio, Texas.

| Esteban y Angélica | Ignacio y Ana | Claudia y Teresa | Raúl y Gloria |

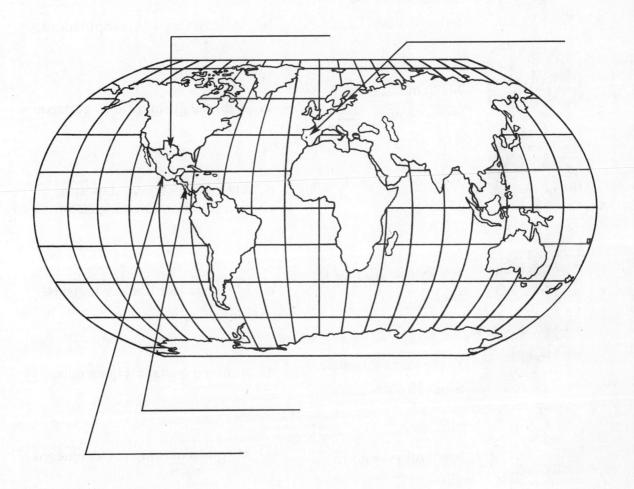

Realidades Ⓐ

Capítulo 1A

Nombre _____

Fecha _____

Hora _____

VIDEO

¿Comprendes?

Actividad 2

Match the characters with the activities they like to do or do not like to do.

1. Me llamo Ignacio y tengo 17 años. _____

a. Me gusta escuchar música también. Pero me gusta más hablar por teléfono.

2. Yo me llamo Ana y tengo 15 años. _____

b. Me gusta usar la computadora.

3. Me llamo Claudia y tengo 16 años. _____

c. A mí me gusta tocar la guitarra.

4. Y yo soy Teresa. Tengo 15 años. _____

d. Me gusta practicar deportes, correr y montar en bicicleta.

5. Soy Esteban. Tengo 15 años. _____

e. Me gusta leer libros y revistas.

6. Yo me llamo Angélica y tengo 16 años. _____

f. A mí me gusta ir a la escuela.

7. Soy Raúl y tengo 15 años. _____

g. Me gusta más jugar videojuegos.

8. Me llamo Gloria y tengo 14 años. _____

h. A mí no me gusta ni correr ni montar en bicicleta. A mí me gusta patinar.

Realidades **A**

Capítulo 1A

Nombre _____

Fecha _____

Hora _____

VIDEO

Actividad 3

Decide whether response a, b, or c best describes the characters in each question.

1. When they are outside, what does Ana ask Ignacio? _____
   a. ¿Te gusta hablar por teléfono?
   b. ¿Qué te gusta hacer?
   c. ¿Te gusta tocar la guitarra?

2. Claudia and Teresa live in Mexico. What do they both like to do? _____
   a. pasar tiempo con amigos
   b. jugar videojuegos
   c. usar la computadora

3. What sports do Esteban and Angélica talk about? _____
   a. correr, montar en bicicleta y patinar
   b. esquiar, correr y nadar
   c. jugar al básquetbol, jugar al fútbol y montar en bicicleta

4. Does Raúl like to go to school? _____
   a. Sí. A Raúl le gusta mucho ir a la escuela.
   b. No. No le gusta nada.
   c. Pues… más o menos.

Y, ¿qué más?

Actividad 4

You have just seen and heard what these eight video friends like or do not like to do. Now fill in the blanks below to tell about things that you like to do and do not like to do.

1. Me gusta _____.

2. A mí me gusta más _____.

3. A mí no me gusta _____.

4. A mí no me gusta ni _____.

Actividad 5

You can learn a lot about a person from what he or she likes to do. You will hear two people from each group of three describe themselves. Listen and match the descriptions to the appropriate pictures. Put an *A* underneath the first person described, and a *B* underneath the second person described. You will hear each set of statements twice.

1. Luisa _____ Marta _____ Carmen _____

2. Marco _____ Javier _____ Alejandro _____

3. Mercedes _____ Ana _____ María _____

4. Carlos _____ Jaime _____ Luis _____

5. Isabel _____ Margarita _____ Cristina _____

Nombre _____   Hora _____

Fecha _____

Actividad 6

A group of students from Peru will visit your school. Since your class will be hosting the students, your teacher is trying to match each of you with a visiting student who likes to do the same things as you do. Listen to the questions and write the students' answers in the blanks. Then, write which of the activities you like better. Find out if the student has the same preferences as you do. Follow the model. You will hear each conversation twice.

Modelo	Guillermo: _____*cantar*_____

A mí: ____*Me gusta más bailar*____ .

1. Paco: _____

A mí: _____ .

2. Ana María: _____

A mí: _____ .

3. José Luis: _____

A mí: _____ .

4. Maricarmen: _____

A mí: _____ .

5. Luisa: _____

A mí: _____ .

Realidades Ⓐ

Capítulo 1A

Nombre _____

Hora _____

Fecha _____

AUDIO

Actividad 7

As one of the judges at your school's fall carnival, your job is to mark on the master tic tac toe board the progress of a live tic-tac-toe competition between Team X and Team O.

As each contestant comes to the microphone, you will hear por X or por O to indicate for which team he or she is playing. The contestant has to answer a question about activities in order to claim the square. Listen for the activity mentioned in each question, and put either an X or an O in the box under the picture of that activity.

At the end of this game round, see which team won! You will hear each statement twice.

Who won the game? _____

Realidades Ⓐ

Capítulo 1A

Nombre _____

Fecha _____

Hora _____

AUDIO

Actividad 8

Luisa, the host of your school's radio station talk show, is interviewing four new students. As you listen to the interview, write down one thing that each student likes to do, and one thing that each student does not like to do. You will hear the entire question and answer session repeated. You will hear this conversation twice.

	Armando	Josefina	Carlos	Marta
Likes				
Dislikes				

Actividad 9

As you turn on the radio, you hear a Spanish radio D.J. talking about the "Top Ten Tips" for being happy during this school year. As you listen, match the suggestion to one of the pictures and number them in the order the suggestions were given on the air. Remember to listen for cognates!

a.	b.	c.	d.	e.
# _____	# _____	# _____	# _____	# _____
f.	g.	h.	i.	j.
# _____	# _____	# _____	# _____	# _____

Actividad 10

Students like to do all sorts of activities during their free periods. Look at the picture below and write what each student is saying he or she likes to do. Then say whether or not you like to do those things. Follow the model.

| Modelo | EL PROFESOR: *A mí me gusta trabajar.* |

TÚ: *A mí me gusta trabajar también.*

ESTUDIANTE #1: _____

TÚ: _____

ESTUDIANTE #2: _____

TÚ: _____

ESTUDIANTE #3: _____

TÚ: _____

ESTUDIANTE #4: _____

TÚ: _____

ESTUDIANTE #5: _____

TÚ: _____

ESTUDIANTE #6: _____

TÚ: _____

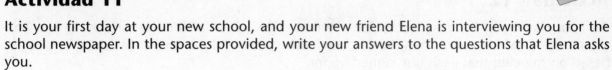

Actividad 11

It is your first day at your new school, and your new friend Elena is interviewing you for the school newspaper. In the spaces provided, write your answers to the questions that Elena asks you.

ELENA: —Buenos días. ¿Cómo estás?

TÚ: —_____

ELENA: —¿Qué te gusta hacer?

TÚ: —_____

ELENA: —¿Te gusta ir a la escuela?

TÚ: —_____

ELENA: —¿Qué te gusta hacer en casa?

TÚ: —_____

ELENA: —¿Te gusta escribir o leer cuentos?

TÚ: —_____

ELENA: —¿Qué más te gusta hacer?

TÚ: —_____

ELENA: —Pues, muchas gracias por la entrevista. Buena suerte.

TÚ: —_____

WRITING

Actividad 12

A. Your classmates have signed up for different clubs. Look at the flyers below to see who signed up for which club. Then, decide how each student might answer the questions below based on the club that each one signed up for.

El Club Educativo	**El Club Deportista**	**EL CLUB MUSICAL**
El club ideal para estudiantes a quienes les gusta ir a la escuela.	El club ideal para estudiantes a quienes les gusta practicar deportes.	El club ideal para estudiantes a quienes les gusta la música.
Actividades:	Actividades:	**ACTIVIDADES:**
• usar la computadora • leer y escribir cuentos • estudiar	• nadar • correr • practicar deportes	• TOCAR EL PIANO O LA GUITARRA • CANTAR • BAILAR
Eduardo _____ Eugenia _____ Esteban _____	Diana _____ Dolores _____ Diego _____	MARICARMEN _____ MANOLO _____ MÓNICA _____

Modelo Eduardo, ¿te gusta tocar la guitarra?

No, no me gusta tocar la guitarra. Me gusta estudiar.

1. Diana, ¿te gusta leer o escribir cuentos?

_____

2. Manolo, ¿qué te gusta hacer?

_____

3. Diego, ¿te gusta ir a la escuela para usar la computadora?

_____

4. Mónica, ¿te gusta nadar o correr?

_____

5. Eugenia, ¿qué te gusta hacer?

_____

B. Now, pick which club you would join and say why. Follow the model.

Modelo _Prefiero el Club Educativo porque me gusta ir a la escuela._

Prefiero el Club _____ porque _____

_____

Actividad 13

A. Write two sentences about things that you like to do, and two sentences about things that you do not like to do. Follow the model.

Modelo *A mí me gusta leer.* _____

No me gusta correr. _____

1. _____

2. _____

3. _____

4. _____

B. Now, use your sentences from Part A to write a letter to your new penpal that will tell her a little bit about you.

```
                                                    29/9/2003

        Saludos,
        _____

        _____

        _____

        _____

        _____

        También _____

        _____

        _____

        _____

                              Un abrazo,

                              _____
```

Realidades (A)

Capítulo 1B

Nombre _____

Hora _____

Fecha _____

VIDEO

Antes de ver el video

Actividad 1

During the video, Teresa, Claudia, Pedro, and Esteban describe each other in e-mails. How would you describe yourself? Below is a list of descriptive words. Check off the words that describe you.

Soy...

☐ artístico, -a   ☐ impaciente   ☐ simpático, -a

☐ atrevido, -a   ☐ inteligente   ☐ sociable

☐ deportista   ☐ ordenado, -a   ☐ talentoso, -a

☐ desordenado, -a   ☐ paciente   ☐ trabajador, -ora

☐ estudioso, -a   ☐ reservado, -a

☐ gracioso, -a   ☐ serio, -a

¿Comprendes?

Actividad 2

Fill in the blanks with the appropriate word or phrase from the bank. You may have to watch the video several times to remember each character well.

misteriosa	reservado	ordenados	inteligente
serio	trabajadora	sociable	
simpática	hablar por teléfono	buena	

1. A Pedro no le gusta ni bailar ni cantar. Es _____.

Pero él escribe: "Soy muy gracioso. No soy muy _____."

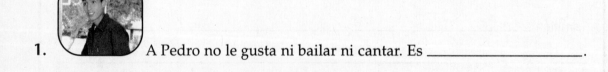

Nombre _____   Hora _____

Fecha _____

2. Teresa, desde un cibercafé en la Ciudad de México, escribe: "Yo soy *Chica*

_____."

3. Ella es la _____ amiga de Claudia.

4. Le gusta _____ , pero no le gusta ir a la escuela.

5. En la computadora, Claudia se llama *Chica* _____.

6. A ella le gusta la escuela; es muy _____, estudiosa

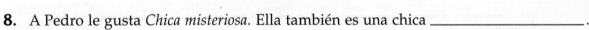

y _____ .

7. También le gustan los chicos inteligentes y _____.

8. A Pedro le gusta *Chica misteriosa*. Ella también es una chica _____.

Realidades Ⓐ

Capítulo 1B

Nombre _____

Hora _____

Fecha _____

VIDEO

Actividad 3

According to Esteban, Pedro is quiet and reserved. Yet, in his e-mail, he writes the opposite. Read what he writes about himself in his e-mail. Then, write what he is really like by filling in the blanks.

> Me llamo Chico sociable. ¡Qué coincidencia! Me gusta
> pasar tiempo con mis amigos... Me gusta escuchar
> música. Según mis amigos soy muy gracioso. No soy muy
> serio.   Escríbeme.

1. *Chico sociable*, el _____ de Esteban, se llama _____ .

2. Según Esteban, él no es un chico _____. Él es _____ .

3. A Pedro no le gusta ni _____ ni _____ .

4. Pedro no es muy _____. Él es muy _____ .

Y, ¿qué más?

Actividad 4

Describe people you know using each of the adjectives from the following list. Follow the model.

paciente	inteligente	sociable	impaciente	deportista

Modelo *La profesora de español es muy inteligente.*

_____

_____

_____

_____

Realidades Ⓐ

Capítulo 1B

Nombre _____

Fecha _____

Hora _____

AUDIO

Actividad 5

You are a volunteer for a service at your school that helps new students meet other new students in order to make the transition easier. People who are interested in participating in this program have left messages describing themselves. Listen as the students describe themselves, and put a check mark in at least two columns that match what each student says. Then write the names of the most well-matched students. You will hear each statement twice.

BUENOS AMIGOS

	CARMEN	PABLO	ANA	ANDRÉS	RAQUEL	JORGE
serio(a)						
reservado(a)						
deportista						
estudioso(a)						
talentoso(a)						
gracioso(a)						
atrevido(a)						
trabajador(a)						
artístico(a)						
sociable						
romántico(a)						

BUENOS AMIGOS:

1. _____ y _____

2. _____ y _____

3. _____ y _____

Realidades Ⓐ

Capítulo 1B

Nombre _____

Fecha _____

Hora _____

AUDIO

Actividad 6

What is your favorite season of the year? Your choice could say a lot about you. Listen as talk-show psychologist Doctor Armando describes people according to their preferred season (**estación preferida**) of the year. What characteristics go with each season? Listen and put a check mark in the appropriate boxes. By the way, is it true what he says about you and your favorite season? You will hear each statement twice.

Mi estación preferida es _____. Según el Dr. Armando, yo soy

_____.

Nombre _____

Hora _____

Fecha _____

AUDIO

Actividad 7

Your Spanish teacher encourages you to speak Spanish outside of class. As you walk down the hall, you hear parts of your classmates' conversations in Spanish. Listen to the conversations and decide whether they are talking about a boy, a girl, or if you can't tell by what is being said. Place a check mark in the appropriate box of the table. You will hear each statement twice.

	#1	#2	#3	#4	#5	#6	#7	#8
(boy)								
(girl)								
?								

Actividad 8

Listen as Nacho describes his ex-girlfriend. How many things do they have in common? Put an *X* on the pictures that show ways in which they are very different and put a circle around the pictures that show ways they are very similar. You will hear each set of statements twice.

1.

2.

3.

4.

5.
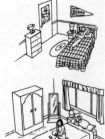

Realidades Ⓐ

Capítulo 1B

Nombre _____

Fecha _____

Hora _____

AUDIO

Actividad 9

Some people say we are what we dream! Listen as Antonieta calls in and describes her dream (**sueño**) to Doctor Armando, the radio talk show psychologist. Draw a circle around the pictures below that match what she dreams about herself.

After you hear Antonieta's call, tell a partner what kinds of things would be in a dream that reveals what you like to do and what kind of person you are. You might begin with "**En mi sueño, me gusta...**". You will hear this dialogue twice.

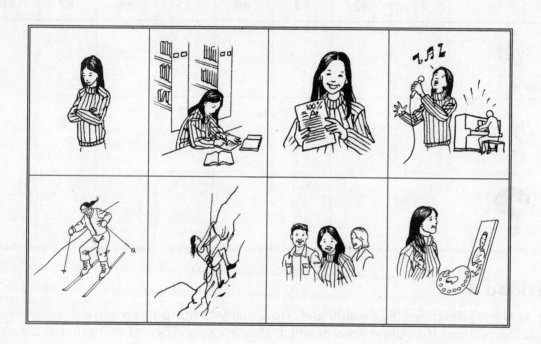

Realidades Ⓐ

Capítulo 1B

Nombre _____

Hora _____

Fecha _____

WRITING

Actividad 10

A. Fill in the words using the art as clues.

1. Marta es una chica _____.

2. Cristina es mi amiga _____.

3. Alicia es muy _____.

4. Isa es una chica _____.

5. Alejandro es muy _____.

6. Carlos es un chico _____.

7. Kiko es _____.

8. Pepe es mi amigo _____.

B. Now, check your answers by finding them in the word search.

```
N E P M V P I Q U U T D
T R A B A J A D O R A E
A S O I D U T S E D G S
L A K U X M A L E A R O
E M D I C Z P P O C A R
N T P A O X O J Z I C D
T I U M N R U F R T I E
O Q K I T E I T E S O N
S M X I E T D G P I S A
A O S L U R M R Y T O D
P T L A E U U J O R H O
A S O C I A B L E A E T
```

Realidades Ⓐ

Capítulo 1B

Nombre _____

Fecha _____

Hora _____

WRITING

Actividad 11

Frida and Diego, who are opposites, are talking on the phone. Frida, the sociable one, is doing all the talking. Using the pictures of the friends below, write what Frida might be saying about herself and about Diego. Follow the models.

Modelo	*Yo soy deportista.*	**Modelo**	*Tú eres paciente.*

1. _____   1. _____

2. _____   2. _____

3. _____   3. _____

4. _____   4. _____

5. _____   5. _____

Actividad 12

Answer the following questions. Be sure to use the definite or indefinite article where appropriate. Follow the model.

Modelo ¿Cómo es tu mamá (*mother*)?

Ella es simpática y graciosa. _____

1. ¿Cómo eres tú?

   _____

2. ¿Cómo es tu profesor(a) de español?

   _____

3. ¿Cómo es tu mejor amigo(a)?

   _____

4. ¿Cómo es el presidente?

   _____

5. ¿Cómo es el director/la directora (*principal*) de tu escuela?

   _____

6. ¿Qué te duele?

   _____

7. ¿Cuál es la fecha de hoy?

   _____

8. ¿Cuál es la fecha del Día de la Independencia?

   _____

9. ¿Cuál es tu estación favorita?

   _____

10. ¿Qué hora es?

   _____

Realidades Ⓐ

Capítulo 1B

Nombre _____

Fecha _____

Hora _____

WRITING

Actividad 13

A reporter for the school newspaper has asked you and several other students in your classroom to submit an article for the paper. The article is about personality traits and activities people like and dislike.

A. Think about your own personality traits. Write four adjectives that describe what you are like and four that describe what you are not like.

SOY

_____

_____

_____

_____

NO SOY

_____

_____

_____

_____

B. Now, write four things that you like to do and four things that you do not like to do.

ME GUSTA

_____

_____

_____

_____

NO ME GUSTA

_____

_____

_____

_____

C. Now, write your article using the information you have compiled about yourself.

_____

_____

_____

_____

_____

_____

_____

_____

_____

Realidades Ⓐ

Capítulo 2A

Nombre _____

Fecha _____

Hora _____

VIDEO

Antes de ver el video

Actividad 1

Think of two of your favorite and two of your least favorite classes. Write the name of each class, when you have it, and why it is your favorite or least favorite.

Clase	Hora	Comentarios

¿Comprendes?

Actividad 2

Claudia had a bad day. Circle the correct answer to explain what happened to her.

1. Claudia tiene un día difícil en el colegio (*high school*). ¿Por qué?
   a. A Claudia no le gusta su colegio.
   b. Claudia no tiene amigos.
   c. Tiene problemas con el horario.
   d. A Claudia no le gustan las matemáticas.

2. ¿En qué hora tiene Claudia la clase de matemáticas?
   a. en la primera hora
   c. en la quinta hora
   b. en la tercera hora
   d. todas las anteriores (*all of the above*)

3. Claudia habla con la persona que hace el horario. ¿Cómo se llama?
   a. Sra. Santoro   b. Sr. López   c. Srta. García   d. Sr. Treviño

4. Para Teresa la clase de inglés es
   a. aburrida.   b. interesante.   c. fantástica.   d. difícil.

5. En la tercera hora Claudia piensa que las matemáticas son aburridas, porque
   a. es el primer día de clases.
   c. tiene seis clases de matemáticas hoy.
   b. la profesora es muy divertida.
   d. no entiende las matemáticas.

Realidades A

Capítulo 2A

Nombre _____

Fecha _____

Hora _____

VIDEO

Actividad 3

Write **cierto** (*true*) or **falso** (*false*) next to each statement.

1. La clase de matemáticas es muy fácil para Claudia. _____

2. Teresa habla con el Sr. Treviño del problema con su horario. _____

3. Teresa y Claudia tienen el almuerzo a la misma hora. _____

4. Teresa tiene la clase de ciencias sociales en la tercera hora. _____

Y, ¿qué más?

Actividad 4

Complete the paragraph with information about your teachers, classes, school, and friends.

El profesor / La profesora que más me gusta es el Sr. / la Sra. _____.

Él / Ella enseña la clase de _____ en la _____ hora y su clase

es muy _____.

Después de la _____ hora tengo el almuerzo. Me gusta mucho porque

puedo estar con _____ y _____ ; ellos / ellas son mis

amigos / amigas.

El director / La directora de mi colegio se llama _____. Él / Ella es muy

_____ y _____.

Actividad 5

You overhear several people in the hall trying to find out if they have classes together this year. As you listen to each conversation, write an *X* in the box under *SÍ* if they have a class together, or under *NO* if they do not. You will hear each conversation twice.

	SÍ	NO
1.	_____	_____
2.	_____	_____
3.	_____	_____
4.	_____	_____
5.	_____	_____

Actividad 6

As you stand outside the school counselor's office, you hear four students trying to talk to him. They are all requesting to get out of a certain class. From the part of the conversation that you hear, write in the blank the class from which each student is requesting a transfer. You will hear each statement twice.

	CLASE	PROFESOR(A)
1.	matemáticas	el profesor Pérez
2.	arte	la profesora Muñoz
3.	español	el profesor Cortez
4.	ciencias sociales	la profesora Lenis
5.	almuerzo	
6.	ciencias	el profesor Gala
7.	educación física	el profesor Fernández
8.	inglés	la profesora Ochoa

1. La clase de _____

2. La clase de _____

3. La clase de _____

4. La clase de _____

Realidades Ⓐ

Capítulo 2A

Nombre

Fecha

Hora

AUDIO

Actividad 7

Emilio, a new student from Bolivia, is attending his first pep assembly! He is eager to make friends and begins talking to Diana, who is sitting next to him. Listen to their conversation. If they have something in common, place a check mark in the column labeled **Ellos**. If the statement only applies to Emilio, place a check mark in the column labeled **Él**. If the statement only applies to Diana, place a check mark in the column labeled **Ella**. **Note:** Be sure you have placed a check mark in ONLY one of the columns for each statement. You will hear the conversation twice.

INFORMACIÓN	ÉL	ELLA	ELLOS
Tiene la clase de español en la primera hora.			
Tiene la clase de español en la segunda hora.			
Tiene una profesora simpática.			
Tiene una profesora graciosa.			
Tiene una clase de arte en la quinta hora.			
Tiene una clase de educación física en la quinta hora.			
Practica deportes.			
Estudia mucho en la clase de matemáticas.			
Es trabajador(a).			
Tiene mucha tarea.			
Tiene almuerzo a las once y media.			

AUDIO

Actividad 8

Listen as four people talk about what they do during the day. There will be some things that all four people do and other things that not all of them do. Fill in the grid with a check mark if the person says he or she does a certain activity. Also, fill in the **Yo** column with a check mark for the activities that you do every day. You will hear each set of statements twice.

	EVA	DAVID	RAQUEL	JOSÉ	YO

Nombre _____ Hora _____

Fecha _____

AUDIO

Actividad 9

You and your family are considering hosting a student from Costa Rica for a semester. Before you make the decision, you want to know a little about the student. Listen to part of a recording that the students from Costa Rica made for your class. Use the grid to keep track of what each of the students says. You will then use this information to decide which student would be the most compatible for you and your family. You will hear each set of statements twice.

Estudiante	Característica(s) de la personalidad	Clase favorita	Actividades favoritas
JORGE			
LUZ			
MARCO			
CRISTINA			

Which student is most like you? _____

Realidades Ⓐ

Capítulo 2A

Nombre _____

Fecha _____

Hora _____

WRITING

Actividad 10

Your classmates are curious about your schedule at school. Using complete sentences, tell them what classes you have during the day. Follow the model.

Modelo *Yo tengo la clase de inglés en la segunda hora.*

1. _____

2. _____

3. _____

4. _____

5. _____

6. _____

7. _____

Actividad 11

Answer the following questions using the subject pronoun suggested by the pictures. Follow the model.

Modelo ¿Quiénes usan la computadora?

Ellos usan la computadora.

¿Quién habla con Teresa?

1. _____.

¿Quién habla con Paco?

2. _____

3. ¿Quiénes hablan?

_____.

4. ¿Cómo es el Sr. García?

_____.

5. Ana, ¿tienes la clase de arte en la primera hora?

Sí, _____.

Ana

6. ¿Cristina y yo somos muy buenas amigas?

Sí, _____.

Cristina   Yo

Actividad 12

A new student at your school has come to you for information about how things work at your school and what your day is like. Answer the student's questions truthfully in complete sentences. Follow the model.

> Modelo   ¿La secretaria habla mucho por teléfono?
>
> _Sí, ella habla mucho_ _____ .

1. ¿Estudias inglés en la primera hora?

   _____

2. ¿Quién enseña la clase de matemáticas?

   _____

3. ¿Necesito un diccionario para la clase de arte?

   _____

4. ¿Cantas en el coro (*choir*)?

   _____

5. ¿Pasas mucho tiempo en la cafetería?

   _____

6. ¿Uds. practican deportes en la clase de educación física?

   _____

7. ¿Los estudiantes usan las computadoras en la clase de ciencias naturales?

   _____

8. ¿Uds. bailan en la clase de español?

   _____

9. ¿Los profesores tocan el piano en la clase de música?

   _____

10. ¿Los estudiantes hablan mucho en la clase de francés?

    _____

Realidades Ⓐ

Capítulo 2A

Nombre _____

Hora _____

Fecha _____

WRITING

Actividad 13

A. List two classes that you have, when you have them, and who the teacher is.

	Clase	Hora	Profesor(a)
1.	_____	_____	_____
2.	_____	_____	_____

B. Now, write complete sentences about whether or not you like each class from Part A. Make sure to tell why you do or do not like each class.

Clase 1: _____

_____

_____

_____

Clase 2: _____

_____

_____

_____

C. Now, using the information from Parts A and B, write a paragraph about one of the classes. Make sure to tell the name of the class, when you have it, and who the teacher is. You should also describe your teacher, tell what you do in class, and say whether or not you like the class.

_____

_____

_____

_____

_____

_____

_____

Nombre _____   Hora _____

Fecha _____   **VIDEO**

Antes de ver el video

Actividad 1

Look around your classroom and make a list of five items that you see. Then, describe their location. Follow the model.

COSA	DÓNDE ESTÁ
Modelo *la papelera*	*debajo del reloj*
1.	
2.	
3.	
4.	
5.	

¿Comprendes?

Actividad 2

Using the screen grabs as clues, answer the following questions with the correct information from the video.

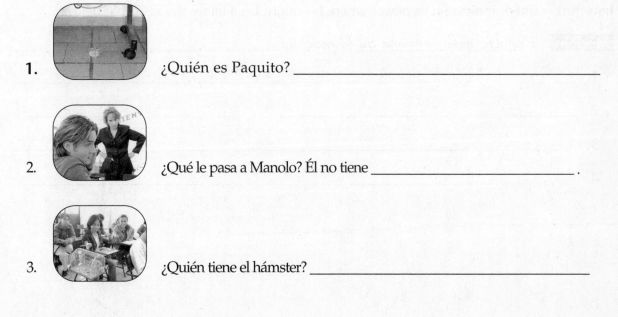

1.   ¿Quién es Paquito? _____

2.   ¿Qué le pasa a Manolo? Él no tiene _____ .

3.   ¿Quién tiene el hámster? _____

4. Los estudiantes están en _____ .

5. ¿Para qué es el hámster? Es para _____ .

Actividad 3

Next to each phrase, write the name of the character who said it in the video.

1. "¿Un ratón en la clase de ciencias sociales? ¡Imposible!"   _____

2. "¡No es un ratón! Es mi hámster."   _____

3. "Señorita, necesito hablar con usted más tarde."   _____

4. "Carlos, no tengo mi tarea."   _____

5. "¡Aquí está! Está en mi mochila."   _____

6. "Paquito, mi precioso. Ven aquí. ¿Estás bien?"   _____

Y, ¿qué más?

Actividad 4

Imagine that Paquito is running around in your classroom. Using the prepositions that you have just learned, indicate four places where he might be. Follow the example below.

Modelo   *Paquito está encima de la mochila.* _____

1. _____

2. _____

3. _____

4. _____

Nombre

Hora

Fecha

Actividad 5

As you look at the picture, decide whether the statements you hear are **ciertos** or **falsos**. You will hear each statement twice.

1. cierto falso	**6.** cierto falso	**11.** cierto falso
2. cierto falso	**7.** cierto falso	**12.** cierto falso
3. cierto falso	**8.** cierto falso	**13.** cierto falso
4. cierto falso	**9.** cierto falso	**14.** cierto falso
5. cierto falso	**10.** cierto falso	**15.** cierto falso

Actividad 6

Tomás suddenly realizes in the middle of his science class that the diskette with his entire class project on it is missing! He asks several people if they know where it is. Listen as different people tell Tomás where they think his diskette is. In the timeline, write what classroom he goes to and where in the classroom he looks, in the order in which you hear them. You will hear this conversation twice.

	Susana	Antonio	Noé	Sr. Atkins
Classroom				
Location in room				

Where did Tomás eventually find his diskette? _____

Actividad 7

It's time to take the Spanish Club picture for the yearbook, but there are several people who have still not arrived. Andrés, the president, decides to use his cell phone to find out where people are. As you listen to the first part of each conversation, complete the sentences below with the information he finds out. For example, you might write: **Beto está en el gimnasio.** You will hear each dialogue twice.

1. Los dos profesores de español _____.

2. Javier _____.

3. Alejandra y Sara _____.

4. Mateo _____.

5. José y Antonieta _____.

Realidades Ⓐ

Capítulo 2B

Nombre

Hora

Fecha

AUDIO

Actividad 8

One of your classmates from Spanish class is working in a store that sells school supplies. She overhears a customer speaking Spanish to his father, and decides to try out her Spanish. As she asks him what he wants to buy, she discovers that he never wants just one of anything. As the customer tells your classmate what he wants, write the items on the sales receipt below. Use the pictures below to calculate the price of his purchases. You will hear each conversation twice.

¿QUÉ NECESITA COMPRAR?	PRECIO
Modelo *Tres bolígrafos*	*$6.00*
1.	
2.	
3.	
4.	
5.	
6.	

Realidades Ⓐ

Capítulo 2B

Nombre _____

Fecha _____

Hora _____

AUDIO

Actividad 9

Listen to two friends talking outside the door of the Spanish Club meeting. They want to go to the meeting, but they are afraid they won't remember everyone's names. Look at the drawing. In the grid, write in the name of the person who is being described. You will hear each dialogue twice.

(A)	(B)	(C)
(D)	(E)	(F)

Nombre _____

Hora _____

Fecha _____

WRITING

Actividad 10

After your first day of school, you are describing your classroom to your parents. Using the picture below, tell them how many of each object there are in the room. Follow the model.

| Modelo | *Hay un escritorio en la sala de clases.* _____ |

1. _____

2. _____

3. _____

4. _____

5. _____

6. _____

7. _____

WRITING

Actividad 11

You are describing your classroom to your Spanish-speaking pen pal. Using complete sentences and the verb **estar**, tell what is in your room and where each item is located. Follow the model.

Modelo	*Hay una mesa en la clase. Está al lado de la puerta.*

1. _____

2. _____

3. _____

4. _____

5. _____

6. _____

7. _____

8. _____

Actividad 12

Answer the following questions about things you have for school. Use the pictures as a guide. Follow the model.

Modelo	¿Qué hay en la mochila?

_____ *Hay unos lápices y bolígrafos. También hay una calculadora y dos* _____
libros: el libro de matemáticas y el libro de inglés. _____

Nombre _____ Hora _____

Fecha _____

1. ¿Qué hay en la clase de ciencias sociales?

_____

_____

_____

_____

2. ¿Qué hay encima del escritorio? ¿Y al lado? ¿Y detrás?

_____

_____

_____

_____

Nombre _____

Hora _____

Fecha _____

WRITING

Actividad 13

The two rooms pictured below were once identical, but Sala 2 has been rearranged. Look at each picture carefully. Circle seven items in Sala 2 that are different from Sala 1. Then, write sentences about how Sala 2 is different. Follow the model.

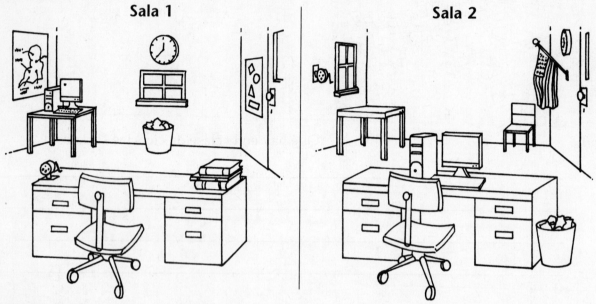

Sala 1   Sala 2

Modelo *En la sala 2 no hay libros encima del escritorio.*

1. _____

_____

2. _____

_____

3. _____

_____

4. _____

_____

5. _____

_____

6. _____

_____

7. _____

_____

Nombre _____ Hora _____

Fecha _____

VIDEO

Antes de ver el video

Actividad 1

What do you like to eat for breakfast and lunch? Fill in the chart with that information.

Desayuno	Almuerzo

¿Comprendes?

Actividad 2

Think about the foods Rosa believes people in the United States eat for breakfast. What do Tomás and Raúl really eat?

1. ¿Qué come Tomás para el desayuno?

   Tomás bebe _____ y come _____ para el desayuno.

2. Y, ¿qué come Raúl?

   Raúl bebe _____ y _____ , come _____ , y a

   veces también come un _____ .

Nombre _____   Hora _____

Fecha _____

Actividad 3

Although Rosa makes a big breakfast for Tomás that day, the family does not eat very much regularly. Answer the questions below.

1. ¿Quién prepara el desayuno? _____

2. Lorenzo: "Es mucha comida, ¿no? _____ ,

   _____ , _____ , _____ ,

   _____ ..." Rosa: "En los Estados Unidos, todos comen mucho en el

   desayuno."

3. Lorenzo: "Nosotros nunca comemos mucho en el desayuno,

   Rosa. Mira, yo sólo bebo un _____ y a veces como

   un _____ ."

4. Según Rosa, en los Estados Unidos comemos huevos, salchichas,

   tocino y pan tostado en el desayuno y _____

   _____ en el almuerzo.

Y, ¿qué más?

Actividad 4

Do you recall what you wrote in **Actividad** 1 about foods that you like to eat? Now that you have heard people in Costa Rica talk about what they eat, write down three questions of your own to ask a classmate about food. With a partner, ask your questions and compare answers.

¿ _____ ?

¿ _____ ?

¿ _____ ?

Nombre _____ Hora _____

Fecha _____

AUDIO

Actividad 5

You are helping out a friend at the counter of Restaurante El Gaucho in Argentina. Listen to the orders and record the quantity of each item ordered by each customer in the appropriate box of the chart. You will hear each conversation twice.

RESTAURANTE EL GAUCHO

El almuerzo	Cliente 1	Cliente 2	Cliente 3	Cliente 4
Ensalada				
Hamburguesa				
Hamburguesa con queso				
Sándwich de jamón y queso				
Perro caliente				
Pizza				
Papas fritas				
Refresco				
Té helado				
Galletas				

Nombre _____

Hora _____

Fecha _____

Actividad 6

While working at the Hotel Buena Vista, you need to record breakfast orders for room service. Use the grid to make your report. First, listen carefully for the room number and write it in the appropriate box. Then write in the time requested. Finally, put a check mark next to each item ordered by the person in that room. You will hear each set of statements twice.

HOTEL BUENA VISTA

Número de habitación (room number)				
Hora de servicio				
Jugo de naranja				
Jugo de manzana				
Cereal				
Pan tostado				
Huevos				
Jamón				
Tocino				
Salchichas				
Yogur de fresas				
Café				
Café con leche				
Té				

Realidades Ⓐ

Capítulo 3A

Nombre _____

Fecha _____

Hora _____

AUDIO

Actividad 7

You are waiting in line at a restaurant counter. You hear people behind you talking about your friends. Listen carefully so you can figure out whom they're talking about. Pay close attention to verb and adjective endings. Put a check mark in the column after each conversation. You will hear each set of statements twice.

	Carlos	Gabriela	Carlos y sus amigos	Gabriela y sus amigas
1.	_____	_____	_____	_____
2.	_____	_____	_____	_____
3.	_____	_____	_____	_____
4.	_____	_____	_____	_____
5.	_____	_____	_____	_____
6.	_____	_____	_____	_____
7.	_____	_____	_____	_____

Actividad 8

Listen as actors from a popular Spanish soap opera are interviewed on the radio program called "**Las dietas de los famosos**" (*Diets of the Famous*). As you listen, write **sí** if the person mentions that he or she eats or drinks something most days. Write **no** if the person says that he or she never eats or drinks the item. You will hear this conversation twice.

	Lana Lote	Óscar Oso	Pepe Pluma	Tita Trompo

Nombre _____   Hora _____

Fecha _____

	Lana Lote	Óscar Oso	Pepe Pluma	Tita Trompo
(strawberries)				
(bananas)				
(hamburgers)				
(french fries)				
(hot dogs)				
(cookies)				
(salad)				
(tea)				
(water bottle)				
(coffee)				

Nombre _____ Hora _____

Fecha _____

Actividad 9

Listen as the woman at the table next to you tries to help a child order from the menu. As you listen, check off the items on the menu that the child says he likes and those he dislikes. Then in the space provided, write what you think would be an "acceptable" lunch for him. You will hear this conversation twice.

le gusta								
no le gusta								

Un almuerzo bueno para Beto es _____

_____ .

Nombre _____

Hora _____

Fecha _____

WRITING

Actividad 10

You have decided to help your parents by doing the food shopping for the week. Your friend Rodrigo is helping you make the shopping list. Complete the conversation below using the picture and your own food preferences.

RODRIGO: ¿Qué hay de beber?

TÚ: _____

RODRIGO: ¿Quieres (*do you want*) algo más?

TÚ: _____

_____

RODRIGO: ¿Qué hay de comer para el desayuno?

TÚ: _____

RODRIGO: ¿Qué más quieres, entonces?

TÚ: _____

_____

RODRIGO: ¿Qué hay para el almuerzo?

TÚ: _____

RODRIGO: ¿Y quieres algo más?

TÚ: _____

_____

RODRIGO: ¿Y qué frutas necesitan?

TÚ : _____

Realidades (A)

Capítulo 3A

Nombre _____

Fecha _____

Hora _____

WRITING

Actividad 11

Describe each of the following scenes using as many **-er** and **-ir** verbs as you can. Use complete sentences.

_____

_____

_____

yo

Ana y yo

tú

los estudiantes

_____

_____

_____

Nombre _____ Hora _____

Fecha _____

WRITING

Actividad 12

In anticipation of your arrival in Spain next week, your host sister writes to ask you about your favorite foods. Complete your response below with sentences using the verbs **gustar** and **encantar**.

Estimada Margarita:

Gracias por su carta. Hay muchas comidas que me gustan. Para el desayuno,

_____. También

_____. Pero no

_____.

Pero me encanta más el almuerzo. Por ejemplo, _____

_____. También

_____. Pero no _____

_____.

¿Y a ti? ¿Te gustan las hamburguesas? ¿ _____

_____? ¿_____

_____? ¿_____

_____?

Nos vemos en una semana.

Un fuerte abrazo,

Melinda

WRITING

Actividad 13

The school nurse is teaching a class on nutrition and asks everyone to fill out a survey about what he or she eats. Using complete sentences, write your responses below.

1. ¿Qué comes y bebes en el desayuno?

_____

_____

_____

_____

_____

2. ¿Qué come y bebe tu familia en el almuerzo?

_____

_____

_____

_____

_____

3. ¿Qué comida te encanta?

_____

_____

_____

_____

_____

Nombre _____ Hora _____

Fecha _____

Antes de ver el video

Actividad 1

Think about the typical diet of a teenager. Which foods are healthy choices and which ones are not? Make a list of five foods in each category.

Comida buena para la salud ☺   **Comida mala para la salud** ☹

_____   _____

_____   _____

_____   _____

_____   _____

_____   _____

¿Comprendes?

Actividad 2

Write the name of the person from the video who made each statement.

1. "El café de aquí es muy bueno."   _____

2. "No, no; un refresco no; un jugo de fruta."   _____

3. "En Costa Rica, un refresco es un jugo de fruta."   _____

4. "Yo hago mucho ejercicio..."   _____

5. "Aquí en San José, todos caminamos mucho."   _____

6. "... aquí una soda no es una bebida; es un restaurante." _____

7. "Me encanta el gallo pinto."   _____

Realidades Ⓐ

Capítulo 3B

Nombre _____

Hora _____

Fecha _____

VIDEO

Actividad 3

Answer the questions.

1. ¿Qué es muy importante para Costa Rica?

_____

2. Según Raúl, ¿qué es bueno de Costa Rica?

_____

3. Según Tomás, ¿qué es bueno para la salud?

_____

4. ¿Qué hacen todos en San José?

_____

5.  ¿Qué más hacen en San José?

_____

6.  ¿Qué es una *soda* en Costa Rica?

_____

Nombre _____

Hora _____

Fecha _____

Y, ¿qué más?

Actividad 4

Tomás was confused because he learned that **un refresco** was a soft drink. However, in Costa Rica **un refresco** is fruit juice. Can you think of any examples of English words that have a different meaning depending on where in the United States you go? What are their different meanings?

_____

_____

_____

_____

_____

_____

_____

Actividad 5

Listen to a radio announcer as he interviews people at the mall about their lifestyles. Pay close attention to the things that they say they do and eat. What in their lifestyles is good or bad for their health? Match what they say to the pictures below. Then write the corresponding letter in the appropriate column. You will hear this conversation twice.

ACTIVIDADES

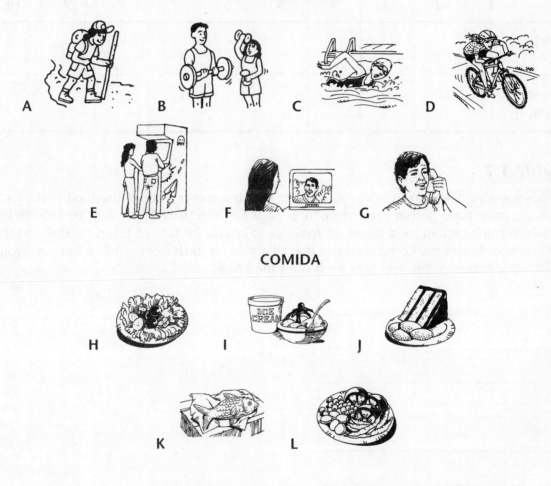

A   B   C   D

E   F   G

COMIDA

H   I   J

K   L

	Bueno para la salud ☺	**Malo para la salud** ☹
1. Mariana	_____	_____
2. Jorge	_____	_____
3. Luz	_____	_____
4. Nacho	_____	_____

Realidades Ⓐ

Capítulo 3B

Nombre _____

Hora _____

Fecha _____

AUDIO

Actividad 6

Listen as students in a health class in Costa Rica present a list of the "dos and don'ts" of staying healthy. Which are **consejos lógicos** (*logical advice*) and which are **consejos ridículos** (*ridiculous advice*)? Place a check mark in the appropriate box of the chart. You will hear each set of statements twice.

	1	2	3	4	5	6	7	8	9	10
Consejo lógico										
Consejo ridículo										

Actividad 7

A Spanish-speaking telemarketer calls your home to interview you about the food preferences of teens. He must have gotten your name from your Spanish teacher! He asks you to tell him whether you think certain food items are **malo** or **sabroso**. Be sure to listen carefully so that you will be able to use the correct form of the adjective for each item. Write what you would say in the spaces below. You will hear each question twice.

1. _____

2. _____

3. _____

4. _____

5. _____

6. _____

7. _____

8. _____

9. _____

10. _____

Nombre _____ Hora _____

Fecha _____

AUDIO

Actividad 8

In an effort to improve food in the school cafeteria, students are asked to anonymously call in their opinions about school food. You are asked to chart the responses of the Spanish-speaking students. As you listen to their opinions, fill in the grid. If they say something positive about a particular menu item, put a plus sign in the appropriate column; if they say something negative, put a minus sign in the column. You will hear each set of statements twice.

1										
2										
3										
4										
5										

Actividad 9

Listen as people call in to ask Dr. Armando their health questions on his radio program **"Pregunte al doctor Armando."** While you listen to their questions and Dr. Armando's advice (**consejo**), fill in the chart below. Do you agree with his advice? You will hear this conversation twice.

NOMBRE	¿LA PREGUNTA?	EL CONSEJO
1. Beatriz		
2. Mauricio		
3. Loli		
4. Luis		

Realidades A

Capítulo 3B

Nombre _____

Fecha _____

Hora _____

WRITING

Actividad 10

A. The school nurse has compiled information on what everyone eats and is now telling you which foods are good for your health and which are not. Remember what you wrote for her survey? List the items you eat on a daily basis. Be sure to use words from the previous chapter as well as ones from this chapter.

_____ _____ _____

_____ _____ _____

_____ _____ _____

_____ _____ _____

B. Now, use the nutrition pyramid shown and what you know about a well-balanced diet to fill in what the nurse would say. Follow the model.

Modelo *Los espaguetis son buenos para la salud. Ud. debe comer mucho pan y*
muchos cereales.

1. _____

_____

2. _____

_____

3. _____

_____

4. _____

_____

Nombre _____ Hora _____

Fecha _____

WRITING

Actividad 11

Write your opinions of the following foods. Use the correct forms of the following adjectives in your sentences.

bueno	malo	sabroso	divertido
malo para la salud		bueno para la salud	
	interesante		horrible

Modelo   *Las uvas son sabrosas.* _____

1. _____

2. _____

3. _____

4. _____

5. _____

6. _____

7. _____

8. _____

WRITING

Actividad 12

Below you see three groups of friends sitting at tables in a cafeteria. Describe the people and items at each table.

Mesa 1:

_____

_____

_____

_____

Mesa 2:

_____

_____

_____

_____

Mesa 3:

_____

_____

_____

_____

Realidades Ⓐ

Capítulo 3B

Nombre _____

Fecha _____

Hora _____

WRITING

Actividad 13

Write a letter to your Spanish-speaking pen pal about a restaurant that you and your parents like to go to for dinner. Tell what you and your family members normally eat and drink, what the food is like, and what the waiters (**camareros**) are like.

Estimado(a) _____ :

_____

_____

_____

_____

_____

_____

_____

_____

_____

_____

_____

_____

_____

_____

_____

_____

_____

_____

Un abrazo,

_____

Nombre _____

Fecha _____

Hora _____

VIDEO

Antes de ver el video

Actividad 1

Think of activities you do at different times during the week. Make a list of four activities you do during the week and then four activities you do during the weekend.

Actividades durante la semana

_____

_____

_____

_____

Actividades durante el fin de semana

_____

_____

_____

_____

¿Comprendes?

Actividad 2

Javier has just moved to a new high school in Spain, and he is sitting by himself. Ignacio, Elena, and Ana try to find out more about him. What do they do, and what do they learn? Write **cierto** (*true*) or **falso** (*false*) next to each statement.

1. El estudiante nuevo es un poco reservado. _____

2. Él se llama Gustavo. _____

3. Él es de Salamanca. _____

4. Todos los días va a la biblioteca después de las clases. _____

5. Los tres amigos van a hablar con él. _____

6. A Javier le gusta practicar deportes. _____

Realidades Ⓐ

Capítulo 4A

Nombre

Fecha

Hora

VIDEO

7. A veces, él prefiere ir al cine a ver películas. _____

8. A él no le gusta hablar con su amigo Esteban de San Antonio. _____

Actividad 3

What do the new friends do after class? Fill the blanks with complete sentences.

Nuevos amigos	¿Adónde va después de las clases?
1. Javier	
2. Ignacio	
3. Elena	
4. Ana	

Y, ¿qué más?

Actividad 4

What do you do after school every day? What do you sometimes do, and what do you never do at all? Write a short paragraph about your afterschool activities, following the example below.

Modelo   *Yo voy a mi trabajo todos los días en el centro comercial. A veces,*
voy con una amiga al cine después del trabajo. Nunca voy al gimnasio
durante la semana.

_____

_____

_____

Nombre _____ Hora _____

Fecha _____

AUDIO

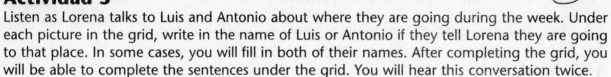

Actividad 5

Listen as Lorena talks to Luis and Antonio about where they are going during the week. Under each picture in the grid, write in the name of Luis or Antonio if they tell Lorena they are going to that place. In some cases, you will fill in both of their names. After completing the grid, you will be able to complete the sentences under the grid. You will hear this conversation twice.

lunes							
martes							
miércoles							
jueves							
viernes							
sábado							
domingo							

1. Luis y Antonio van al (a la) _____ el _____.

2. También van al (a la) _____ el _____.

Nombre _____ Hora _____

Fecha _____

AUDIO

Actividad 6

You are volunteering as a tour guide during the upcoming Hispanic Arts Festival in your community. To make sure you would be able to understand the following questions if a visitor were to ask them, write the number of the question under the correct picture that would correspond to a logical response. You can check your answers to see if you're ready to answer visitors' questions during the Festival. You will hear each question twice.

Actividad 7

Your friend Miguel calls his mother from your house to give her an update on his plans for the day. Just from listening to his side of the conversation, you realize that his mother has LOTS of questions. What does she ask him, based on Miguel's answers? Choose from the following:

A. ¿Adónde vas?

D. ¿Cómo es tu amigo?

B. ¿Con quiénes vas?

E. ¿Por qué van?

C. ¿Cuándo vas?

You will hear each set of statements twice.

1. _____ 2. _____ 3. _____ 4. _____ 5. _____

Realidades Ⓐ

Capítulo 4A

Nombre _____

Fecha _____

Hora _____

AUDIO

Actividad 8

The yearbook staff is identifying students' pictures for the yearbook. Look at the pictures from the class trip to Mexico. Listen to the conversations and write the names of Arturo, Susi, Gloria, Martín, David, Eugenia, Enrique, and Lucía under the correct pictures. You will hear each dialogue twice.

Actividad 9

Listen as a radio interviewer talks to Maricela, a young woman from Spain, about her city that was once home to the **Reyes** Fernando and Isabel. You will learn why it is such a popular tourist spot. After listening, answer the questions below. You will hear this conversation twice.

1. Maricela es de
   a) Madrid.   b) Aranjuez.   c) Barcelona.

2. La ciudad es famosa por
   a) el pescado.   b) el helado.   c) las fresas.

3. Los turistas van
   a) al palacio.   b) a las montañas.   c) a la playa.

4. La ciudad de Maricela está a unos _____ minutos de Madrid.
   a) quince   b) treinta   c) cincuenta

5. Las comidas típicas son
   a) pizza y espaguetis.   b) fresas y pasteles de manzana.   c) pollo y judías verdes.

6. Maricela va _____ para pasar tiempo con los amigos.
   a) al parque   b) al cine   c) a las montañas

Nombre _____

Hora _____

Fecha _____

WRITING

Actividad 10

While on a hike one day, you stumble upon a "Wheel of the Future." When you spin this wheel, you will land on a picture of a place. The wheel will send you to that place if you tell it when you want to go and what you plan to do there. Write what you would tell the wheel for each place. Follow the model.

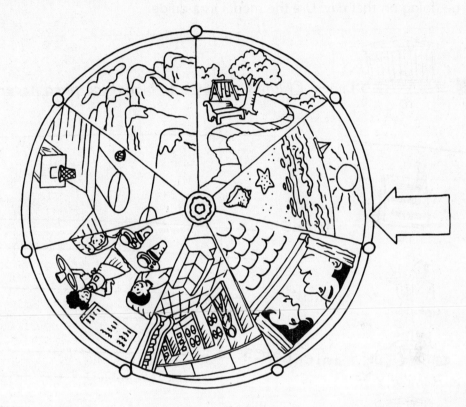

Modelo _Voy a la playa el viernes para nadar._

1. _____

2. _____

3. _____

4. _____

5. _____

6. _____

7. _____

Realidades Ⓐ

Capítulo 4A

Nombre _____

Fecha _____

Hora _____

WRITING

Actividad 11

You are having a surprise party for your best friend next weekend, and you need to know where your family and friends are going to be this week so that you can get in touch with them to make plans. Below is a planner containing information on everyone's plans for the week. Using the pictures to help you, write where your friends and family will be and what they will be doing on that day. Use the model as a guide.

Modelo YO

Lunes: _El lunes yo voy a la biblioteca para hacer la tarea._

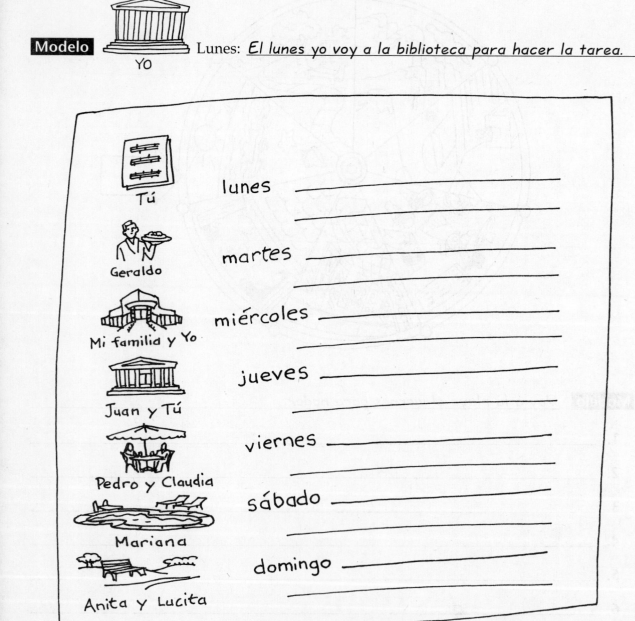

Tú	lunes _____
Geraldo	martes _____
Mi familia y Yo	miércoles _____
Juan y Tú	jueves _____
Pedro y Claudia	viernes _____
Mariana	sábado _____
Anita y Lucita	domingo _____

Actividad 12

You are a contestant on a game show. The host of the show has given you these answers. Write the corresponding questions.

Modelo   El catorce de febrero

¿Cuándo es el Día de San Valentín? _____

1. El primer presidente de los Estados Unidos

   _____

2. Al norte (*north*) de los Estados Unidos

   _____

3. Usamos esta cosa para conectar al Internet.

   _____

4. Muy bien, gracias. ¿Y tú?

   _____

5. Vamos a la tienda para comprar frutas.

   _____

6. Las personas que enseñan las clases

   _____

7. Usamos estas partes del cuerpo para ver.

   _____

Actividad 13

A. Write four complete sentences that tell about places you and a friend go to on the weekend.

1. _____

2. _____

3. _____

4. _____

Realidades **A**

Capítulo 4A

Nombre _____

Hora _____

Fecha _____

WRITING

B. Now, use your sentences from Part A to write a paragraph telling with whom you go to these places, what the places are like, and what you do when you are there.

_____

_____

_____

_____

_____

_____

_____

_____

_____

_____

_____

_____

_____

Antes de ver el video

Actividad 1

Think of activities you like to do. Here is a list of six activities. Rank them in order from your favorite to your least favorite, with 1 as your favorite and 6 as your least favorite.

_____ ir a bailar   _____ ir al cine a ver películas

_____ nadar   _____ montar en bicicleta

_____ estudiar en la biblioteca   _____ ir de compras al centro comercial

¿Comprendes?

Actividad 2

Ignacio, Javier, Elena, and Ana are playing soccer at the park. Who makes each statement? Write the name of the person who says each item on the line.

1. "Mañana juego al tenis con mis primos."   _____

2. "Yo también estoy muy cansada y   _____
   tengo mucha sed."

3. "Prefiero otros deportes, como el fútbol."   _____

4. "¿Sabes jugar también al vóleibol?"   _____

5. "También me gusta ir de pesca."   _____

6.   "Puedes bailar conmigo…"   _____

7. "Lo siento. No sé bailar bien."   _____

8. "Voy a preparar un pastel fabuloso."   _____

Nombre _____ Hora _____

Fecha _____

VIDEO

Actividad 3

Look at the activities below, and circle the ones you saw or heard about while watching the video. Then, write the ones that Elena can do well on the lines below.

jugar al fútbol	jugar al tenis	ir de cámping	ir de pesca
ir a las fiestas	ver el partido	jugar al vóleibol	
caminar en el parque	jugar al fútbol americano		practicar deportes
ir al concierto	preparar un pastel	jugar al béisbol	jugar al golf
jugar al básquetbol	bailar y cantar	tomar refrescos	

_____

_____

Y, ¿qué mas?

Actividad 4

Imagine that Ignacio, Javier, Elena, and Ana want you to join them in their various activities. What answers might you give them? Respond to their invitations with some of the phrases from the video, or make up your own responses from what you have learned. Follow the model.

Modelo ¿Quieres jugar al fútbol en el parque?

Sí, quiero jugar al fútbol en el parque, pero no juego muy bien.

1. ¿Puedes jugar al tenis mañana?

_____

2. Oye, juegas muy bien al vóleibol. ¿Puedes jugar más tarde?

_____

3. ¿Quieres ir con nosotros a la fiesta esta noche?

_____

4. ¿Sabes bailar?

_____

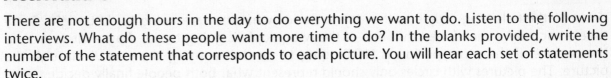

Actividad 5

There are not enough hours in the day to do everything we want to do. Listen to the following interviews. What do these people want more time to do? In the blanks provided, write the number of the statement that corresponds to each picture. You will hear each set of statements twice.

Actividad 6

After listening to each of the following statements, decide if you think the excuses given are believable (**creíble**) or unbelievable (**increíble**). Be prepared to defend your answers with a partner after making your decisions. You will hear each set of statements twice.

EXCUSAS, EXCUSAS

	Creíble	Increíble		Creíble	Increíble
1.	☐	☐	5.	☐	☐
2.	☐	☐	6.	☐	☐
3.	☐	☐	7.	☐	☐
4.	☐	☐	8.	☐	☐

Realidades Ⓐ

Capítulo 4B

Nombre _____

Fecha _____

Hora _____

AUDIO

Actividad 7

Listen to the following couple as they try to decide what they are going to do tonight. Every time an activity is mentioned that one of the two people is going to do, draw a circle around the picture. If the other person is NOT going to do that activity, draw an X through the picture. The pictures with circles only should represent what both people finally decide to do. You will hear each conversation twice.

Actividad 8

Listen as a radio program host interviews a fitness expert, doctora Benítez, about the best way to get in shape. Listen to the **entrevista** (*interview*), and choose the best answer to the questions below. You will hear this conversation twice.

1. ¿En qué es experta la doctora Benítez?

   a) deportes   b) cocinar   c) música   d) ejercicio y nutrición

2. Según la doctora, ¿cuántos minutos de ejercicio debes hacer todos los días?

   a) una hora   b) quince minutos   c) treinta minutos

3. Según Miguel, ¿por qué no puede hacer mucho ejercicio?

   a) Es demasiado perezoso.   b) Está muy ocupado.   c) Está triste.

4. ¿Qué es divertido para Miguel?

   a) jugar al tenis   b) ver la tele   c) jugar al fútbol

5. Después de jugar, ¿qué no debemos comer?

   a) cereales   b) frutas y verduras   c) pasteles

Nombre _____ Hora _____

Fecha _____ **AUDIO**

Actividad 9

Your Spanish teacher always encourages you to speak Spanish to your classmates outside of class. In order to do that, you and your friends agreed to talk on the phone and/or leave messages on each other's answering machines for at least a week. Listen to the messages your friends have left on your answering machine today. Based on the messages, decide a) where the person wants to go; b) what the person wants to do; c) what time the person wants to go. Use the chart below to record the information. You will hear each set of statements twice.

	¿Adónde quiere ir?	¿Qué quiere hacer?	¿A qué hora quiere ir?
Justo			
Eva			
José			
Margarita			
Pedro			

Nombre _____

Hora _____

Fecha _____

Actividad 10

A. Read the following announcements of upcoming events in Madrid. Underneath each announcement, write whether or not you are going to each event and why or why not.

UNA NOCHE DE ÓPERA ITALIANA

PRESENTANDO a **JOSÉ CARRERAS** en el Auditorio Nacional de Música, Madrid

el viernes a las siete de la noche

PARTIDO DE FÚTBOL

REAL BETIS CONTRA REAL MADRID

el domingo a las dos de la tarde en el Estadio Santiago Bernabeu

---

Fiesta Deportiva

¿Te gusta practicar deportes? ¿Eres atlético?

Ven a mi fiesta deportiva y puedes jugar varios deportes con muchas personas.

La fiesta es desde el viernes a las cinco de la tarde hasta el lunes a las cinco de la mañana.

B. Now, in the spaces below, write whether five people you know are going to any one of the events and why or why not. Follow the model.

Modelo   *Mi amiga Ana va al partido de fútbol porque le gusta mucho el fútbol.*

Mi amigo Ronaldo no va al concierto porque no le gusta la ópera.

1. _____

2. _____

3. _____

4. _____

5. _____

Actividad 11

Every time a classmate asks Eugenio if he wants to do something fun, he declines and gives a different excuse. In the spaces below, write the question that each classmate asks and Eugenio's varying answers. Follow the model.

Modelo

—¿Vas a levantar pesas conmigo?

—No, no puedo levantar pesas porque me duele la cabeza.

1. —¿_____?

—No, _____.

2. —¿_____?

—No, _____.

3. —¿_____?

—No, _____.

4. —¿_____?

—No, _____.

5. —¿_____?

—No, _____.

6. —¿_____?

—No, _____.

7. —¿_____?

—No, _____.

Nombre _____ Hora _____

Fecha _____

WRITING

Actividad 12

When put in the right order, each set of blocks below will ask a question. Unscramble the blocks by writing the contents of each block in the blank boxes. Then, answer the questions in the space provided.

1.

JUEG	DE	EPOR	OS	F UÉ	D	AS	L

INES	¿A	Q	TES	NA?	SEMA

_____

_____

2.

¿A	Q	MIGO	TES	US	A	JUEG	UÉ	D

S?	AN	T	EPOR

_____

_____

3.

GA?	L ES	FAVO	¿CUÁ	RITO	JUE

RTE	UIÉN	Y Q	TU	DEPO

_____

_____

Nombre _____ Hora _____

Fecha _____ **WRITING**

Actividad 13

You are having a mid-semester party.

A. First, fill in the invitation below with the information about your party.

FIESTA DE MEDIO SEMESTRE

Lugar: _____

Hora: _____

Comida: _____

_____

RSVP: _____

B. Since you don't have everyone's mailing address, you have to e-mail some people about the party. Write your e-mail below. In addition to inviting them, tell them what activities you will have at the party, and where your house is (**está cerca de la biblioteca**, etc.).

Estimados amigos:

_____

_____

_____

_____

_____

_____

_____

¡Me gustaría ver a todos en la fiesta!

Un fuerte abrazo,

_____

Song Lyrics

These are the lyrics for the songs that appear on the Canciones CD.

Track 01

ALEGRE VENGO

Alegre vengo de la montaña
De mi cabaña que alegre está
A mis amigos les traigo flores
De las mejores de mi rosal
A mis amigos les traigo flores
De las mejores de mi rosal

Ábreme la puerta
Ábreme la puerta
Que estoy en la calle
Y dirá la gente
Que esto es un desaire
Y dirá la gente
Que esto es un desaire

A la sarandela, a la sarandela
A la sarandela, de mi corazón
A la sarandela, a la sarandela
A la sarandela, de mi corazón

Allá dentro veo, allá dentro veo
Un bulto tapado
No sé si será un lechón asado
No sé si será un lechón asado
A la sarandela...

Track 02

LA MARIPOSA

Vamos todos a cantar,
vamos todos a bailar
la morenada.

Vamos todos a cantar,
vamos todos a bailar
la morenada.

Con los tacos,
con las manos.
¡Viva la fiesta!

Con los tacos,
con las manos.
¡Viva la fiesta!

Track 03

ERES TÚ

Como una promesa eres tú, eres tú
como una mañana de verano;
como una sonrisa eres tú, eres tú;
así, así eres tú.

Toda mi esperanza eres tú, eres tú,
como lluvia fresca en mis manos;
como fuerte brisa eres tú, eres tú
así, así eres tú.

[estribillo]
Eres tú como el agua de mi fuente;
eres tú el fuego de mi hogar.
Eres tú como el fuego de mi hoguera;
eres tú el trigo de mi pan.

Como mi poema eres tú, eres tú;
como una guitarra en la noche.
Todo mi horizonte eres tú, eres tú;
así, así eres tú.

Eres tú como el agua de mi fuente;
eres tú el fuego de mi hogar.
Algo así eres tú;
algo así como el fuego de mi hoguera.
Algo así eres tú;
Mi vida, algo, algo así eres tú.

Eres tú como el fuego de mi hoguera;
eres tú el trigo de mi pan.
Algo así eres tú;
algo así como el fuego de mi hoguera.
Algo así eres tú;

Track 04

LA CUCARACHA

[estribillo]
La cucaracha, la cucaracha,
ya no quiere caminar,
porque no tiene, porque le falta
dinero para gastar.

La cucaracha, la cucaracha,
ya no quiere caminar,
porque no tiene, porque le falta
dinero para gastar.

Una cucaracha pinta
le dijo a una colorada:
Vámonos para mi tierra
a pasar la temporada.

Una cucaracha pinta
le dijo a una colorada:
Vámonos para mi tierra
a pasar la temporada.

La cucaracha, la cucaracha,
ya no quiere caminar,
porque no tiene, porque le falta
dinero para gastar.

Todas las muchachas tienen
en los ojos dos estrellas,
pero las mexicanitas
de seguro son más bellas.

Todas las muchachas tienen
en los ojos dos estrellas,
pero las mexicanitas
de seguro son más bellas.

La cucaracha, la cucaracha,
ya no quiere caminar,
porque no tiene, porque le falta
dinero para gastar.

Una cosa me da risa,
Pancho Villa sin camisa,
ya se van los carrancistas,
porque vienen los villistas.

Una cosa me da risa,
Pancho Villa sin camisa,
ya se van los carrancistas,
porque vienen los villistas.

La cucaracha, la cucaracha,
ya no quiere caminar,
porque no tiene, porque le falta
dinero para gastar.

Track 05

EL CÓNDOR PASA

Al cóndor de los Andes despertó
una luz,
una luz,
de un bello amanecer, amanecer.

Sus alas en lo alto extendió
y bajó,
y bajó,
al dulce manantial, para beber.

La nieve de las cumbres brilla ya
bajo el sol, el día y la luz.
La nieve de las cumbres brilla ya
bajo el sol, el día y la luz,
del bello amanecer, amanecer.

Al cóndor de los Andes despertó
una luz,
una luz,
de un bello amanecer, amanecer.

Sus alas en lo alto extendió
y bajó,
y bajó,
al dulce manantial, para beber.

La nieve de las cumbres brilla ya
bajo el sol, el día y la luz.
La nieve de las cumbres brilla ya
bajo el sol, el día y la luz,
del bello amanecer, amanecer.

Track 06

ASÓMATE AL BALCÓN

Asómate al balcón para que veas mi
parranda
Asómate al balcón para que veas
quien te canta
Asómate al balcón para que veas tus
amigos
Asómate al balcón
Formemos un vacilón

Asómate, asómate, asómate, asómate

Yo sé que quieres dormir
Pero así es la Navidad
Y si tú no te levantas
Te sacamos de la cama
Aunque tengas que pelear

Asómate al balcón para (se repite)

¡Asómate, asómate, asómate, asómate!

Track 07

LA BAMBA

Para bailar la bamba, para bailar la bamba
se necesita una poca de gracia,
una poca de gracia y otra cosita
y arriba y arriba,
y arriba y arriba y arriba iré,
yo no soy marinero, yo no soy marinero,
por ti seré, por ti seré, por ti seré.

Bamba, bamba...

Una vez que te dije, una vez que te dije
que eras bonita, se te puso la cara,
se te puso la cara coloradita
y arriba y arriba,
y arriba y arriba y arriba iré,
yo no soy marinero, yo no soy marinero,
soy capitán, soy capitán, soy capitán.

Bamba, bamba...

Para subir al cielo, para subir al cielo
se necesita una escalera grande,
una escalera grande y otra chiquita
y arriba y arriba,
y arriba y arriba y arriba iré,
yo no soy marinero, yo no soy marinero,
por ti seré, por ti seré, por ti seré.

Bamba, bamba...

Track 08

HIMNO DEL ATHLETIC DE BILBAO

Tiene Bilbao un gran tesoro
que adora y mima con gran pasión.
Su club de fútbol
de bella historia,
lleno de gloria,
mil veces campeón.

Athletic, Athletic club
de limpia tradición,
ninguno más que tú
lleva mejor blasón.

Del fútbol eres rey,
te llaman el león
y la afición el rey
del fútbol español.

Cantemos pues los bilbainitos,
a nuestro club con gran amor,
para animarle con nuestro himno,
el canto digno del Alirón.

¡Alirón! ¡Alirón!
el Athletic es campeón.

Track 9

PARA ROMPER LA PIÑATA

Echen confites y canelones
pa' los muchachos
que son comilones.
Castaña asada, piña cubierta,
pa' los muchachos que van a la puerta.

Ándale, Lola,
no te dilates

con la canasta
de los cacahuates.

En esta posada
nos hemos chasqueado,
porque la dueña
nada nos ha dado.

Track 10

PIÑATA

Dale, dale, dale,
no pierdas el tino,

mide la distancia
que hay en el camino.

Track 11

LAS MAÑANITAS

Éstas son las mañanitas
que cantaba el Rey David,
pero no eran tan bonitas
como las cantan aquí.

[estribillo]
Despierta, mi bien, despierta,
mira que ya amaneció,
ya los pajarillos cantan,
la luna ya se metió.

Despierta, mi bien, despierta,
mira que ya amaneció,
ya los pajarillos cantan,
la luna ya se metió.

Si el sereno de la esquina
me quisiera hacer favor,
de apagar su linternita
mientras que pasa mi amor.

[estribillo]
Despierta, mi bien, despierta,
mira que ya amaneció,
ya los pajarillos cantan,
la luna ya se metió.

Despierta, mi bien, despierta,
mira que ya amaneció,
ya los pajarillos cantan,
la luna ya se metió.

Track 12

DE COLORES

De colores, de colores se visten los
campos en la primavera.
De colores, de colores son los pajaritos
que vienen de afuera.
De colores, de colores es el arco iris
que vemos salir.
Y por eso los grandes amores de
muchos colores me gustan a mí.
Y por eso los grandes amores de
muchos colores me gustan a mí.

De colores, de colores brillantes y finos
se viste la aurora.
De colores, de colores son los mil
reflejos que el sol atesora.
De colores, de colores se viste el
diamante que vemos lucir.
Y por eso los grandes amores de
muchos colores me gustan a mí.
Y por eso los grandes amores de
muchos colores me gustan a mí.

Track 13

MÉXICO LINDO Y QUERIDO

Voz de la guitarra mía,
al despertar la mañana,
quiere cantar su alegría
a mi tierra mexicana.

Yo le canto a tus volcanes,
a tus praderas y flores
que son como talismanes
del amor de mis amores.

México lindo y querido
si muero lejos de ti
que digan que estoy dormido
y que me traigan aquí.

México lindo y querido
si muero lejos de ti
que digan que estoy dormido
y que me traigan aquí.

Voz de la guitarra mía,
al despertar la mañana,
quiere cantar su alegría
a mi tierra mexicana.

Yo le canto a tus volcanes,
a tus praderas y flores
que son como talismanes
del amor de mis amores.

México lindo y querido
si muero lejos de ti
que digan que estoy dormido
y que me traigan aquí.

México lindo y querido
si muero lejos de ti
que digan que estoy dormido
y que me traigan aquí.

Track 14

MI CAFETAL

Porque la gente vive criticándome
Me paso la vida sin pensar en ná

Porque la gente vive criticándome
Paso la vida sin pensar en ná

Pero no sabiendo que yo soy el hombre
Que tengo un hermoso y lindo cafetal

Pero no sabiendo que yo soy el hombre
Que tengo un hermoso y lindo cafetal

Yo tengo mi cafetal
Y tú ya no tienes ná...

Yo tengo mi cafetal
Y tú ya no tienes ná...

Colombia mi tierra bonita

Nada me importa que la gente diga
Que no tengo plata que no tengo ná

Nada me importa que la gente diga
Que no tengo plata que no tengo ná

Pero no sabiendo que yo soy el hombre
Que tengo un hermoso y lindo cafetal

Pero no sabiendo que yo soy el hombre
Que tengo un hermoso y lindo cafetal

Yo tengo mi cafetal
Y tú ya no tienes ná..

Yo tengo mi cafetal
Y tú ya no tienes ná..

Track 15

MARÍA ISABEL

La playa estaba desierta,
el mar bañaba tu piel,
cantando con mi guitarra
para ti, María Isabel.

La playa estaba desierta,
el mar bañaba tu piel,
cantando con mi guitarra
para ti, María Isabel.

[estribillo]
Toma tu sombrero y póntelo,
vamos a la playa, calienta el sol.

Toma tu sombrero y póntelo,
vamos a la playa, calienta el sol.

Chiri biri bi, poro, pom, pom.
Chiri biri bi, poro, pom, pom.
Chiri biri bi, poro, pom, pom.
Chiri biri bi, poro, pom, pom.

En la arena escribí tu nombre
y luego yo lo borré
para que nadie pisara
tu nombre: María Isabel.

En la arena escribí tu nombre
y luego yo lo borré
para que nadie pisara
tu nombre: María Isabel.

[estribillo]
Toma tu sombrero y póntelo,
vamos a la playa, calienta el sol.

Toma tu sombrero y póntelo,
vamos a la playa, calienta el sol.

Chiri biri bi, poro, pom, pom.
Chiri biri bi, poro, pom, pom.
Chiri biri bi, poro, pom, pom.
Chiri biri bi, poro, pom, pom.

La luna fue caminando,
bajo las olas del mar;
tenía celos de tus ojos
y tu forma de mirar.

La luna fue caminando,
bajo las olas del mar;
tenía celos de tus ojos
y tu forma de mirar.

[estribillo]
Toma tu sombrero y póntelo,
vamos a la playa, calienta el sol.

Toma tu sombrero y póntelo,
vamos a la playa, calienta el sol.

Chiri biri bi, poro, pom, pom.
Chiri biri bi, poro, pom, pom.
Chiri biri bi, poro, pom, pom.
Chiri biri bi, poro, pom, pom.

Track 16

LA GOLONDRINA

A donde irá veloz y fatigada,
la golondrina que de aquí se irá,
allí en el cielo se mirará angustiada,
sin paz ni abrigo que dio mi amor.

Junto a mi pecho allí hará su nido,
En donde pueda la estacion pasar,
También yo estoy en la región perdida.
¡Oh cielo santo! Y sin poder volar.

También yo estoy en la región perdida.
¡Oh cielo santo! Y sin poder volar.

Junto a mi pecho allí hará su nido,
En donde pueda la estacion pasar,
También yo estoy en la región perdida.
¡Oh cielo santo! Y sin poder volar.

Track 17

¡VIVA JUJUY!

Vamos con ese bailecito

Adentrito cholo

¡Viva Jujuy!
¡Viva la Puna!
¡Viva mi amada!
¡Vivan los cerros
pintarrajeados
de mi quebrada...!

¡Viva Jujuy!
¡Viva la Puna!
¡Viva mi amada!
¡Vivan los cerros
pintarrajeados
de mi quebrada...!

De mi quebrada
humahuaqueña...

No te separes
de mis amores,
¡tú eres mi dueña!

La, lara, rara, rara

No te separes
de mis amores,
¡tú eres mi dueña!

Dos, dos y se va la otrita

Adentro

Viva Jujuy
y la hermosura
de las jujeñas!
Vivan las trenzas
bien renegridas
de mi morena!

Viva Jujuy
y la hermosura
de las jujeñas!
Vivan las trenzas
bien renegridas
de mi morena!

De mi morena
mal pagadora

No te separes
de mis amores
¡tú eres mi dueña!

La, lara, rara, rara

No te separes
de mis amores
¡tú eres mi dueña!

Track 18

ADIÓS MUCHACHOS

Adiós muchachos compañeros de mi vida,
barra querida, de aquellos tiempos.
Me toca a mí hoy emprender la retirada,
debo alejarme de mi buena muchachada.

Adiós, muchachos,
ya me voy y me resigno,
contra el destino nadie la talla.
Se terminaron para mí todas las farras.
Mi cuerpo enfermo no resiste más.

Dos lágrimas sinceras
derramo en mi partida
por la barra querida
que nunca me olvidó.
Y al darle a mis amigos
mi adiós postrero
les doy con toda el alma
mi bendición.

Adiós muchachos compañeros de mi vida,
barra querida, de aquellos tiempos.
Me toca a mí hoy emprender la retirada,
debo alejarme de mi buena muchachada.

Adiós, muchachos,
ya me voy y me resigno,
contra el destino nadie la talla.
Se terminaron para mí todas las farras.
Mi cuerpo enfermo no resiste más.